FAKE
MISSED
CONNECTIONS

FAKE

MISSED

CONNECTIONS

Divorce, Online Dating, and Other Failures

A MEMOIR BY

BRETT FLETCHER LAUER

SOFT SKULL PRESS • NEW YORK

This is a work of nonfiction. In some cases events have been compressed. Names of individuals have been changed to protect their privacy. Dialogue in the work has been reconstructed to the best of the author's recollection.

Library of Congress Cataloging-in-Publication Data is available.
ISBN 978-1-59376-660-3

Cover design by Kelly Winton
Interior design by Elyse Strongin, Neuwirth & Associates

SOFT SKULL PRESS
New York, NY
www.softskull.com

Printed in the United States of America

FOR MY MOTHER
AND FOR GRETCHEN

Passing stranger! you do not know how longingly I look
  upon you,
You must be he I was seeking, or she I was seeking, (it comes
  to me, as of a dream,)
I have somewhere surely lived a life of joy with you,
All is recall'd as we flit by each other, fluid, affectionate,
  chaste, matured,
You grew up with me, were a boy with me, or a girl with me,
I ate with you, and slept with you—your body has become not
  yours only, nor left my body mine only,
You give me the pleasure of your eyes, face, flesh, as we pass—
  you take of my beard, breast, hands, in return,
I am not to speak to you—I am to think of you when I sit
  alone, or wake at night alone,
I am to wait—I do not doubt I am to meet you again,
I am to see to it that I do not lose you.

—WALT WHITMAN,
"To a Stranger," *Leaves of Grass*

1

This is what I am trying to say: I was in no condition to have paid closer attention to plot development. There were no flash-bulb memories pausing time, creating a mental photograph of how sunlight fell in a pattern on the parquet floor, individual facial expressions, what I was wearing, or the particular geometry of where bodies were located in the apartment's floor plan. I've requested all the mental and visual impressions in the library of my brain, like an interlibrary loan—*The Book of Devastating Phone Calls & Their Aftermath* (153.1BFL)—only to learn the book has been pulled from the shelf and remaindered. I have only the frag-ments of conversations, the scrapbooks, the digital debris, and the patchwork of letters saved. I revisit and reread them. I look at them over and over, hoping if I stare at them long enough it becomes something like being there again, like remembering, and thus, once relived innumerable times, becomes solidly the stuff of a past. The phone was ringing. The phone rang. I answered it.

We were living in Oakland, on the border of Berkeley, where the neighborhood began its shift from bungalows carefully crafted in a shabby chic aesthetic to buildings run down by economic factors. I was depressed and could barely leave our apartment. If we were out of milk, I drank my coffee black, spooned the dry breakfast flakes into my mouth. If I managed to leave I checked the front door ten times, knowing each time it would be securely locked. The outside world was oppressive, the streets populated with the unfamiliar eyes of others looking through me and sensing my fears. Fear wasn't my best friend, rather my only friend. Halfway to the train, I'd turn back to check the lock an eleventh time.

I opened the door, inspected each knob on the gas stove, waved my hand before the outlet to ensure the coffeepot was unplugged, and pointed a finger at each cat, an obsessive compulsion manifested to create order, as if the physical gesture could trick my mind into acknowledging the cats hadn't slipped past me and out the front door. I said aloud, "One cat, two cats." I closed the door. I opened it again; there they were as I pointed. "One cat, two cats." If I made it to the train, I put on my earphones and pressed play. Or I put on my earphones to appear preoccupied enough to avoid commuter small talk, the obligation to provide the wayward stranger with directions. I averted my eyes. I looked sideways. I wore a nondescript neutral colored sweatshirt, the hood up in order to appear more menacing from a distance. Anything to get moving properly, rise with enough gusto to get out of the house and order a sandwich, rent a movie, and have a conversation with the cashier at the coffee shop, but one brief enough not to give the wrong impression.

My wife Nina and I sat in our living room. It was less than a week before we left to visit her parents and then embark on the annual Christmas cruise to Mexico with my in-laws. Indistinguishable days at sea, the hours of each day to be marked by meals—a breakfast buffet of wet eggs and burnt bacon, a midday snack of nachos or grilled hot dogs and French fries, a five-course dinner (formal attire required), and a 24-hour self-service soft ice cream machine—all said, on average, to add a pound a day to each traveler. Somewhere onboard, I was told, there would be a gym, not that I would use it. A trip filled with indifferent shuffleboard, karaoke with grandparents in the "community" lounge that at 11 PM promptly transformed, assisted by strobe lights and a fog machine, into a "club" named something like The Cove. Teenagers, twentysomethings with glow-in-the-dark drinking-age wristbands, and inevitably me crowded in and dancing to Nelly's "Hot in Herre." I'd taken a version of this cruise before. It advertised exactly three port destinations in which one could pay an additional fee to swim with dolphins or scuba dive. We wouldn't. We would wander the historic section of town or sit for half of a day on a crowded beach where I'd have to disguise my pale skin in a T-shirt.

We had waited until the last minute to secure a pet-sitter and had to forego comparison shopping. And so we found ourselves slightly annoyed and embarrassed to be paying $125 a day for a stranger to collect the few bills and catalogs from our mailbox, deposit them on the coffee table, then perform the required task of petting our cats. There was nothing to be done about it. A middle-aged woman sat across from us. I want to say she wore Crocs and a polar fleece, but this is how I've come to describe everyone in the Bay Area: a blur of stock footage reduced to fair-trade granola, a breezy disposition, and a yoga mat. I'm not positive, but I don't believe she maintained eye contact when I interrupted to confess we didn't feed our cats grain-free food. I can say with certainty I observed the cat-sitter's mouth twist with disapproval when I admitted we left a bowl of kibble out at all times, rather than providing a structured meal schedule.

Everything I did in California inspired this feeling of being judged—the look of a cashier when I packed our groceries with a brown bag, or when, instead of carrying my wife's box of tampons two blocks home, I asked for a plastic bag. My friends left piss to brew in my toilet under the conservationist theory "If it's yellow, let it mellow." I double-bagged groceries from spite and allowed myself guilt-free extra-long showers in which, well after the last lather of soap was rinsed off, I did nothing but lean my forehead against the cool tile while hot water slid down the drain. Once, I plucked a dead leaf from the jade on the windowsill, placed it in the toilet, and flushed twice.

So it was then in our living room, prompted by this Californian condescension and not necessarily by an overprotective love towards my cats, that I took the liberty to articulate my every whim to our sitter: "Here is the leopard printed carrying case. Here is the catnip cigar. Hold your hand exactly two feet from the ground as I'm demonstrating to you now, so Ruby, the black–and–white cat, can rub her head against your opened palm. Here is the laser pointer; please take care that the beam should never touch their body, their paws, as it may confuse their limited notions regarding the physical world."

Two hours later, the cat-sitter long gone, the phone was ringing in our kitchen. I answered it.

"You don't know me. My name is Sophie Reynolds. What I have to tell you is difficult." Her voice reminded me of a nurse's, a professional stranger, and I imagined my mother in a hospital across the country, imagined this nurse in a white hallway with gray doors, wearing white Keds on a linoleum floor, surrounded by fluorescent lights, calling to inform me my mother had died in a drunk driving accident or she was in a coma, and it was uncertain if and when she would wake.

That was what I anticipated, what my family history had prepared for me. Not this: "Your wife is having an affair with my husband. It's caused some trouble in my marriage and I thought you should know." What can one say? Dumbfounded. A lump expanding somewhere in the throat, I managed "Thanks" and hung up the phone.

"Who was that?" Nina was on the couch as I walked across the room to the closet. "Sophie Reynolds." I opened the closet. "Do you have anything you want to tell me?" Silence. I grabbed a coat, or sweater, or sweatshirt. "Do you have anything you want to tell me?" More silence. I closed the closet door and casually put on the garment to maintain a sense of composure as I moved towards the front door. "She said you were having an affair with her husband." I paused; I opened the door, walked out into the morning. It happened that suddenly. I opened the door. I walked out into the sun.

I went straight to the market for a pack of cigarettes, my first in a year. The first cigarette was a task needing completion: confused and in shock, light-headed and slightly ill, the influx of toxins to my bloodstream added to the mixture of psychological stimulants circulating through my body. My body adjusted, began to compensate, the initial spike to the system leveled out, and I began to feel more normal. I remembered to exhale, the aura of bright light closing in on my field of vision receded; I looked at my hand and there it was, shaking. The cloud of shapes in the distance came into focus and there was a man on the corner wearing a multi-colored poncho and a faded Santa Claus hat ringing a bell. I felt his eyes watching me. The bell rang like a metronome marking a normal heart rate. I chain-smoked four cigarettes before I called my brother Simon. Sitting on the stoop of the Oakland Public Library, the fucking sun absurdly shining, I could only speak the most necessary words: "Nina cheated on me."

The day after our wedding, in Nina's parents' living room, Nina cried uncontrollably on the couch. I wanted to believe it was a fit, a state that would arrive and depart, a curse bewitching her that I could outwit, kissing her forehead and reversing the effects. There were piles of gifts wrapped in silver and gold with light blue bows, stuffed in multicolored bags with congratulatory fonts announcing "Best of Luck." I held up a stainless steel rice maker, a polished stockpot, waved a fan of checks and hundred-dollar bills to make her laugh, to break the crying spell. I conducted a fake conversation with an iridescent knock-off Tiffany lamp shaped like a turtle, a gift from her aunt. "Hello, Mr. Turtle. Welcome to the family."

She couldn't stop crying. Her mother rubbed her back, stroked her hair. Nina's anxiety never seemed to manifest itself as a dull dread in the bones, as a momentary pulling of the duvet over her head as the morning alarm rang. It was always inconsolable, always crash-and-smolder for days. Her mother seemed to be the only one who could comfort her, since forever, or at least college. In Nina's first semester at junior college, she was overcome with such a degree of uneasiness that her mother attended classes with her. I imagine they sat in the back, both taking notes, fulfilling their requirements. I unwrapped the cellophane around a Williams-Sonoma gift basket from Ted Danson and Mary Steenburgen. Nina had gone to school with Mary's daughter. I licked my lips. "We'll be eating famous pancakes in no time."

Between gasps, Nina explained she was experiencing a delayed reaction to the pressure of the wedding. I wanted to believe her. Post-Matrimony Depression. The day had come and gone. She had been eerily matter-of-fact through the various stages and negotiations of the wedding. There were no pre-wedding jitters, freak-outs over seating arrangements, favors, or obsessively tracking storm patterns to predict the day's weather. What did I know—this could be an unspoken initiation for newlyweds.

Maybe similar episodes happened to everyone and simply weren't spoken of in polite company. It wasn't until my friends began having children that I learned about a mother's hair falling out after birth, shoe sizes changing, the release of feces and fluids during labor. That wasn't discussed in my health classes. I wanted to believe I was being initiated into marriage. For better or for worse. I believed her.

We were scheduled to fly to Dublin in a few hours and it was unclear if we would make the flight, or depart for a honeymoon at all. I'm sure I said things like: "Europe's not going anywhere—we can cancel reservations, postpone for a month, a year; could go to Paris for our five-year anniversary. People do that all the time. We'll have something to look forward to."

Nina called her doctor. A prescription would be sent to her mother, filled by her mother, and sent to us at our hotel in Dublin. A small majority of the honeymoon was then spent calling FedEx offices, navigating languages and procedures to track the pharmaceutical package. In between, we ducked into Irish doorways so Nina could cry. She remained outside of a bookshop while I browsed the aisles—she pleaded for me to go off on my own while she stayed in the hotel room. "You can't do anything to help me." We went to the natural history museum filled with taxidermy animals in large glass vitrines, a claustrophobic collection recalling a nineteenth-century cabinet of wonders. Polar bears stood on hind legs next to ferrets. There was no discernable logic. I waited in line to witness a page of the *Book of Kells* and examined it for too long—the anxious rustle of purses and guidebooks behind me becoming more and more aggressive. I didn't care. I was alone even when I wasn't. I had nowhere to be. I looked at all things stuffed, ancient, and illuminated. I walked on without her.

Her meds arrived in Dublin the day after we had left for Prague. The room in Prague had us sleeping in separate beds. I stretched out and stayed up late rereading Kafka, and Hrabal's *Closely Observed Trains*. Each morning we crossed the Charles Bridge—past gold objects adorning the bodies of saints. I walked as slowly as possible, the Baroque statuary staring back as they had through beheadings, floods, resistance, the hands and hammers of bygone craftsmen. Reading the guidebook in the airport waiting for our departing flight, I discovered the statues were fakes—the originals long ago shipped to museums for proper tourist admissions and safekeeping. Nina's medication arrived in Prague the day after we arrived in Paris. By the time we reached Paris, we were almost enjoying ourselves, and stopped at an Internet café to translate the phrase: "Cancel shipment."

I went home. There was nowhere else to go. Nina wasn't there. I waited. I lay on the shiny tiled kitchen floor blowing smoke out the screen door of our smoke-free building. I ashed into an orange coffee saucer. I waited. Nina didn't sleep at home that night. I don't know where she slept; rather, I know only where she said she slept. A friend's. The nights she did arrive home after work she went directly into the bathroom to change. She closed and locked the door. I was a stranger now, or actually, something worse—she undressed in front of strangers at the gym.

After *The Phone Call*, as I came to call it, Nina told me she had driven over to Sophie Reynolds's house to confront her, yelled at her through the screen door, "How could you do this to Brett?" I was further humiliated. "Don't you understand she did nothing wrong? You were fucking her husband?" Nina told me Sophie had no right to hurt me. "You understand *she* didn't hurt me, *you* did."

There were a few nights leading up to the cruise in which Nina and I stopped arguing long enough to watch a movie, and as the credits scrolled across the screen, we promptly resumed where we left off. "Why are you crying?" Nothing. "Why are you crying? You can't tell me?" I tried to initiate sex. I placed my hand on her inner thigh. *Take pity.* I thought, *this is how people make up, express forgiveness, mark their territory, alleviate the pain.* She insisted on sleeping on the couch, as if at that point the little gestures of penance could set things right. *Fuck you.* At the same time, I didn't want to rest side by side like two acquaintances sharing a motel bed on a business trip, straining not to touch each other.

This was all before Nina avoided seeing me in person, before she avoided speaking with me on the phone, before she requested all communication travel over the Internet's invisible wires in order, I assume, to mediate the discussion and diminish my tone of disgust.

Three months before the wedding my mother visited me in New York to help shop for a tie and black dress shoes. My brothers had informed me of her intentions. It was a nice opening gambit on her part, the pretext of participating in the sartorial matters of my forthcoming wedding, and I would have thought little of it—she visited more than anyone else in the family, and unlike anyone else in our family had actually once, as a teenager, lived in New York. She'd worked at a department store the summer before marrying my father.

I stood under the main DEPARTURES AND ARRIVALS sign at Penn Station. We went to lunch at a large Mexican restaurant in midtown. The waiter crushed an avocado at our table in a large stone mortar that impressed tourists. My mother called it "one of those New York experiences." The waitress offered us Bloody Marys and we drank iced tea. It was at this meal, a last meal of sorts, that she told me she wasn't coming to my wedding.

It should have been a blessing. A generous wedding gift in disguise. Accept it and never think of it again—that's what my brothers told me. My mother was, in effect, asking to be permitted a pass. There was only so much she could manage, and functioning gracefully in close proximity to my father was beyond her abilities. She had refused to attend my brother Simon's wedding a decade before on the same grounds.

Either as a mature adult clearly expressing myself or a child unwilling to understand the limitations of another, I spoke with a calmness unknown to me, explaining my disappointment. "This really isn't an acceptable option. I thought by now you could handle this." It was a measured tone, cultivated in the years since my childhood outbursts and the resulting nodes that had formed on the throat of the youngest of four boys needing to be heard. It was a tone, admittedly, that could have been interpreted condescendingly. Our conversation followed the course of serious discussions with much more at stake than what was actually being discussed—with the gravitational pull of a black hole, they drew in the subjects that were orbiting the perimeter. "Fine, I'll come to the wedding," she said. I told her, "I heard you were drinking again." She looked away.

I will admit, I did what everyone who has been cheated on does. In the days following *The Phone Call,* with a new critical lens, I mentally revisited every phone call or email claiming she was delayed, working late, shopping for a suit for an upcoming conference. Every event attended without me was reconsidered with the worst intentions in mind. I spent a short lifetime searching through everything: the crumpled papers stained with coffee grounds in the trash, all her purses, the pockets of jackets hanging in the closet—ATM receipts, restaurant mints, a ticket stub, red lipstick.

I placed the past under a magnifying glass, each item burning away as I looked at it closely. My brain centered its attention on my extraordinary will to suffer. I discovered no new information, or what I found could not be identified, just as a blood cell under a microscope is a strange amorphous shape, an abstract expressionist network of branches, until the label tells us otherwise. Bacteria, a lilac leaf, a bee antenna. Or worse, with a theory in mind, I couldn't look objectively; each item fit into my new hypothesis. A new version of a person was being created. Each event happened a particular way. It occurred. I experienced it. Done. What was left to do? Break her things, piss in her lingerie drawer, and pawn the ring on eBay? Instead, I did nothing. I cried on the couch or paced the two rooms. She had decided to go on the cruise, and I wasn't going to wait around in our house until she left. I left California; there was no point in both of us staying in our apartment trying not to make eye contact with each other. My older brother Noah offered to fly me out to spend Christmas with him and I accepted the gift.

December 24, 2006
Nina,

I know you've been angry, upset, and disappointed with me. I'm sure I could list a litany of adjectives to represent the distance which has grown between us. Fine, you met someone else. I can only assume you fell in love with him. There's no evidence to contradict this and in fact you've actively refused to placate me; vacancy possesses your face, a ghost of someone else inhabiting the physical body I once identified as you.

For the sake of this email, I'll set aside your decision to leave for your family cruise without me. Even in this state, my mind can identify a number of reasons: a) it is important to save face b) they paid already c) time apart might help clarify this difficult situation d) all of the above. This is the part of my brain which wishes to create a dignified narrative in these undignified times. I can't help thinking I deserve a little more. I deserve a little more than your brief emails: "I arrived in Puerto Vallarta. The weather is fantastic. Time runs out quickly."

I'm just thinking, maybe it would be appropriate to spend a few more pesos and write me something of any substance, or more substance than the remarks you would note on a postcard to a co-worker. Time does run out quickly in foreign Internet cafes and marriages. I know I'm needy; you've expressed how unattractive a quality that is. I should face facts: you're uninterested in communicating with me. Are you writing to Him? I'm certain this is the case, because you continue to act like someone who doesn't regret their actions, someone without a speck of respect towards me. So please don't continue to tell me otherwise. It's unfair. I know where I stand. I know the responsibility I take in this relationship. And I am determined not to be pushed out to sea. The person I fell in love with wouldn't turn her back so easily on me.

Love,
B.

Dear Jess,

Thanks for calling and sorry I didn't pick up. I just can't bring myself to recount everything over and over with everyone. The conversations with Nina have been unthinkable. I mean, imagine. It's impossible to stop my mind from the impulse to ask her the worst possible questions in order to arrive at some perspective or clarity, to satisfy some rational aspect of uncovering any, for lack of a better phrase, need-to-know facts, whatever they might be. But this is the short of it: She told me they had been together three times over a six month period. And since I've already done the math: in June we were married, in August we moved here, and the affair began sometime before our first wedding anniversary. Who knows how long she was considering acting on this before it actually happened. She told me they were together a few times, whatever that means, that once they "made out" in his office; that once after a work event they went back to his place for a drink. "It just happened." She kept saying, again and again. "It just happened. It wasn't planned." I asked her if she used condoms. She looked at me like I was crazy. She told me "It felt exciting, like I was doing something dangerous." "Did you tell him you loved him? Did you talk during sex? Did you? Did you tell him you loved him?" "I don't know. We were just friends; it is something that just happened." "Do you understand anything? Do you understand that friends don't fuck each other? That when you do that it becomes something else? How do you not remember everything? Shouldn't you have been replaying this in your head over and over for months now? Shouldn't you know every last fucking detail? So you would fuck him and then just come home and watch TV with me? How did you get home from his house?" "He called a taxi, but it didn't come. So he drove me home." "He drove you home to our house? What the fuck did you talk about?" "I don't know, movies. I don't know. I loved him. He was my friend." "Did you think about what kind of future you would have with him, what fucking kind of car you would drive?" "I don't know. Yeah, but I knew it wasn't reality." "What was reality?" "Do you think this has been easy for me? You know, I lost a friend." "I'm sorry, that must be very difficult for you. I don't understand. It isn't like you were drunk, that you were both at a bar flirting and judgment flew out the window for a moment." "I don't know." "No, how? Please fucking enlighten me." "I don't know. I must have been in his office talking with him, and went to give him a hug." "Why are you crying now? Oh, do you miss him?" Nothing. "Why are you crying? You aren't going to tell me? Did you love him? Did you LOVE him?" "He was my friend. I cared for him. And now I know guys and girls can't be friends." "You weren't friends. If I hear that word one more time. Do you even want to be with me? Why would you want to be with me?" "Because I care about you." "That's what you said about Richard too. Why would you want to be with me?" "Because I still can't imagine a more perfect person." "You don't make me feel that way." "Yes, I care for him and while I wish I could just run off into the sunset or whatever bullshit, I know I have my own things to work through on my own." And so it went, and eventually I just went to sleep on the couch.

Brett

I'd hated Christmas since my parents' divorce; the holiday split between two households, each year the tense discussions of who was going to be where and for how long, all parties fastidiously keeping track in order to use it at some later point as a justification for anger or hurt feelings. I still wasn't speaking with my mother after I'd asked her to leave my wedding a year and half before. I had flown to Minneapolis and was sitting quietly on the couch when my mother called Noah on Christmas Day. I could hear him whispering in the next room. "I'm not sure. I think he will try to work it out with her. No, he isn't eating. He leaves the day after tomorrow."

We went to a casino on Christmas Day, tried to kill sadness with kitsch, knowing how depressing and false the pretense of celebrating would feel in my current state. At the blackjack table we were quickly up three hundred dollars. Fortunes change. Noah joked, "Just think of it as going to the bank to make a withdrawal." We quit while ahead and walked out past the indoor water park and drove to a Chinese restaurant, where I ordered a bowl of brown rice and ate a third of it. I'd already begun to lose weight, which I found a perverse joy in, hoping Nina might find me more attractive.

I cried on Noah's front porch, the Minneapolis winter falling indifferently. I charted the days in hours that needed to be occupied. I demanded the television wash over me, obsessively replacing and numbing my own drama with one that could be solved. TV justice was a simple formula: the show started with a dead body and ended in an hour with the apprehension of the killer. And dreary details were inevitably left out, things like meals and showers.

I began to keep a journal of thoughts and conversations in a conscious attempt to have a record. I knew how easily I would forget, how events have a way of changing, are conveniently pushed to a hidden cul-de-sac in the brain. I had done it before. I had done it with my mother. Memories of events with no backstory, simple facts I could no longer recall, forgotten, most likely, in the hope they would never intrude on the daily narrative I told myself: *The world is not terrible*. Details became distorted, the gaps widened, until I no longer believed that they mattered. I tied the threads of a history into a bow and gave them away. And here I was again, knowing someday, at some point, I would forget everything, and I would find myself trying to remember.

Flying from Minneapolis to visit friends in New York, I looked out the airplane window and recited facts, all the facts I could remember. The earth is round. It rotates on an axis of twenty-three degrees, towards the east, in the direction I was traveling. It spins at a calculable speed, and is almost a hundred billion miles from the sun. The numbers become too large to understand. It is the same with suffering—when contemplating a disaster, even when the number of victims increases from one to two, we begin to lose interest. I don't think I invented that fact. I may have. In elementary school we were told to imagine the earth the size of a peppercorn, the size of a golf ball, the distance between planets as some amount of football fields stacked nose to nose. We were told to change the scale. It is important to keep records, to document the behavior, or else we resort to staring at the sky for answers. I kept notes because I wanted to be able to return to that feeling, that moment, so that later, when the facts started slipping, there would be documentation I could examine like a detective working a cold case. And so I replayed the events of my suffering. On the airplane I wrote, "Please let this plane fall from the sky in flames."

I'm at a loss for how I arrived anywhere, how one foot was placed in front of the other to arrive at the security check-in with my messenger bag, how I focused my attention to hear the boarding call, found myself in line to board the aircraft. I began writing a letter to my mother. With nothing making sense, I retraced my steps to find out where I went wrong.

Dear Mom,

I know I will not send this, which I just mistyped as "say this." I begin this letter in anticipation of events that may or may not occur. The sky is gray—this is the season when gray skies permanently fix themselves through day and night, when crystalline lights are strung from trees, transforming what was bare into an object the mind holds with fascination. I remind myself to look away.

Our first interval of silence lasted four years, from 1992 to 1996. I'm not positive why you kicked me out. After the divorce settlement, my father gone, you returned to the family house and for a brief interval we were all together under the same roof again. It wouldn't take long before you were shouting at me to "Get the fuck out of this house." It's possible the next morning you would have forgotten. It's possible Simon phoned dad. "Maybe Brett shouldn't stay here in the house with her." I packed my things. Noah, Simon, and I moved in with my father the next day.

This is the season the wind shakes windows. This is the season I anticipate a letter from you, a reminder you continue to exist; a return address telling me you remain in the town I left over a decade ago. I know the trees you see, the train tracks and bridges you cross in your daily routine, whatever that may now be. I know this better than any return address.

The card you sent to me this year, care of Noah's address, read simply: "I don't care about the details and so forth and so on. I just care about my son. Love, Mom." The cards are never empty. I know once I open them that we share something. My fair skin tinted blue, my blond hair, my hands which tremor with no provocation, and your money. When I was thirteen, when I was fourteen, and so forth and so on, each year four or five drugstore cards. Elves surround a snow-covered evergreen. An elephant holds a flower in his trunk. A print of an old willow tree. A Japanese wood-cut wave forever about to crash. They moved with me, kept in a box in a closet or beneath a bed. We haven't spoken in almost two years, since the day of my wedding. I start this letter, which I will not send, because I want to account for you how I have lived.

I've lived in the suburbs of Philadelphia in three different structures; in Pittsburgh in four; in Brooklyn three; in London two; and in the Bay Area two. Not much occurred. The weather in each place was slightly different; the trees exhibited their own characteristics and were related. Hummingbirds in California reminded me of hummingbirds in Virginia where your mother Orpha lived until she was moved to the suburbs of Philadelphia to die in an air conditioned building conveniently situated off a turnpike exit. The body begins to shrink in old age. We transported her back to Virginia in a shoe-sized box in the trunk of your car. In Virginia, she is said to have done the Queen's hair, when the Queen was visiting and staying at the lodge in 1957. Every summer we visited Orpha in Williamsburg can be distilled into a list: tri-corner-hats, knickers, coloring books of the uniforms of the American Revolution, reproductions of the Constitution, a duck pond at a golf course where she would take us to feed Canadian geese. Standing on a bridge, I dropped pieces of week-old bread. I watched the fish fight, wedge themselves between rocks. I wanted the fish to beach themselves in the shallow waters, to watch them feverish with hunger and excitement. I wanted to see if I could trick them into acting against their own welfare. I wanted to watch them die. On one visit, we went on a candlelight ghost walk through the colonial town, each building distinctly remade to be haunted. Orpha held my hand. I carried her charred bones from the trunk of your car to a hole in the ground. Hard earth, damp earth, in the end it doesn't matter; she was placed two feet deep in Virginia soil. Under a green tent I read a poem to strangers. They all told me she was returned home. "You asked me recently why I claim to be afraid of you," Kafka began a letter to his father. It goes on, heartbreakingly, for some forty pages. The letter was given to his mother for delivery, which she failed to do, and returned it unread. "I did not know, as usual, how to answer, partly for the very reason that I am afraid of you, partly because an explanation of my fear would require more details than I could even begin to make coherent in speech. And if now I try to answer in writing it will still be nowhere near complete, because even in writing my fear and its consequences raise a barrier between us and because the magnitude of material far exceeds my memory and understanding."

I concentrate, sit in the dark with eyes closed, a warm feeling centering in the chest. All that passes through my mind are family photographs, stories with details colored in from echoes and echoes of stories. Fallsington, a seat of early Quaker settlement; preschool, a Quaker meetinghouse. I know each day I wept when you dropped me off outside the stone building. I know I sat all day in a corner with a wooden shoe as my learning aid. At the end of the day while I waited for you to arrive, the class played Telephone, a phrase moved from one ear to another, transforming it into another story.

Love,
Brett

The friends I was visiting went to work. I left their apartment and walked the streets of the city they lived in. Quiet house after quiet house. Bare branches set against a bare sky. A stray cat that followed me for a block. I smoked. I walked and listened to sad songs: "Take a forty-five minute shower and kiss the mirror and say, look at me, baby, we'll be fine, all we gotta do is be brave and be kind." I looked at my watch and waited for another day to conclude. I read the entire Internet. I searched for more music to download. Absent of the adjectives needed to express myself, I looked at the All Music Guide, which described the "moods" of the bands in my current rotation as: earnest, melancholy, gloomy, reflective, autumnal, bittersweet, brooding, cold, paranoid, angst-ridden, theatrical, and wintry. I turned the music up. When the playlist was done it would be time for dinner, then three television programs, then time to sleep. I'm going to make it through this year if it kills me.

Noah had asked if I could have made more of an effort. He said I could have demonstrated a commitment to my marriage by getting my driver's license. It was a ridiculous suggestion, or it should have been—it was exactly what Nina had brought up after *The Phone Call*. "I don't know how you could be a good father." She meant I couldn't take care of myself, that I would never leave the apartment, or drive our imaginary kids, Ezra and Lucia, to soccer practice. I hadn't needed a license in New York City, but if I'd shown some initiative in committing to our new life in the Bay Area where we owned a car, things might have progressed differently. Instead I was the perpetual passenger, turning the dial to find a song to listen to. She was exhausted with taking care of me, with my depression and fears. I understood, sympathized—I had felt equally exhausted with her depression and fears while living in New York.

Moving to the Bay Area was not my idea. Nina had been an undergraduate at Berkeley and she believed New York—the pace, the residual anxiety of 9/11, the distance from her family—was the cause of her uneasiness. There were days when I walked her to the door of her office or calmed her down when she called from work crying. She began taking medication, seeing a therapist. Things returned to a relative calmness, but she didn't want to remain in New York much longer. I never wanted to leave. It was part of the deal; I knew this before I proposed. The move to California was talked about with an inevitability that took for granted the sacrifice I would be making. Couples make these decisions. I'm not saying I didn't understand this. I understood this.

In Oakland, months before I had received *The Phone Call*, when she told me she wanted to go to couples counseling, I told her, "I don't have a problem with that." When she told me she stayed late at work because she hated coming home, I began taking antidepressants the next day. But it was already too late. The scenery had shifted for Nina.

I returned home to Oakland on New Year's Eve and took a cab home to our apartment.

December 31, 2006
Nina,

I'm not sure why I bothered looking. Maybe I knew what I would find. I was putting the laundry away in the dresser and I saw the ring box. I should have known what one finds in a ring box. I told myself I was opening the black box to make sure the cat-sitter hadn't stolen my grandmother's ring. I held the box in my palm. It snapped open. My grandmother's ring was safe and still there, and as you know, so were your engagement and wedding rings. Hope you are having fun in Mexico.

Thanks,
B

I placed a slim gift box beneath our miniature Christmas tree. I downloaded the learner's permit handbook and made an appointment to see a therapist at the Psychoanalytic Institute. She would be home from the cruise in a day, and I would be standing in the doorway. *Forgive me. I can overcome my fear of driving, all fears, for you.* I was partially aware at the time—how one is aware the sun will eventually extinguish itself, or each day lived brings death closer—that these last-minute efforts had missed their deadline by months, but that a failure to try was also its own form of failure. It was important to be noble, to be brave, to admit my wrongs. If our marriage was on course to end, I wanted to look back and say I did everything possible to prevent the outcome, that it was, indeed, not on my behalf, that I wasn't the copilot watching the scenery pass and tuning the dial, that it would be Nina's decision.

January 1, 2007
Dear Nina,

I answered the phone today: "Please hold for an important message," and me holding thinking you were calling to say Happy New Year. It was just a collection agency for a person who once lived here. I left behind everything, my friends, my career, to move to California and build from your happiness. I didn't want to be here, but it was important to you, and you were so unhappy in New York. The phone rang and your name came up on my caller ID. When I answer you are not there. You call back and all I can hear is a faint humming. I say: "I can't hear you but it is nice to hear your voice." Disconnected. I go outside to smoke a cigarette, the home phone rang and I ran in to answer it: "Happy New Year from Cal Girls' Basketball."

Thanks,
Brett

My friend Nick drove down from Occidental to check on me and we went to an outdoor mall. I attempted to articulate to him the feeling of returning to my empty apartment. "It's like when I came home for my first winter recess from college—everything was the same but slightly different. Like, we normally had a real Christmas tree, but my father had purchased an artificial one and it took me two days to tell the difference. Or have you ever had to pack up the house of a dead relative? Everything's there, exactly the same as it was the last time you visited, but the objects, only days severed from their owner, are already filled with nostalgia. I think Richard must have been in the house."

Nick's demeanor hinted that he wasn't going to let on if he did or didn't know anything. "You got married young. Things happen. You moved here and she flourished, started going to the gym. This is the best she's looked and felt in her life." Quietly I nodded. I told myself that if I ever found myself on the opposite side of this conversation at a future moment, walking with an anguished friend or complete stranger, to convey the exact opposite sentiment. *This is awful. You'll get through this.* Not even, *Maybe it is for the best* or *What doesn't kill you. . . .* Nick's perspective wasn't driven by cruelty. He had already arrived at an emotional distance, discerned Nina's motivations that, years later, maybe I would come to grasp, but at that moment I could only think he was privy to something I wasn't.

We continued walking, barely speaking under the winter sun and palm trees amid post-holiday shoppers on the prowl for sales. Nick stopped at a taco truck. I didn't order anything. I understood what Nick was trying to explain. There was little I hadn't already analyzed with my brother, or friends, or hopelessly scrawled in an ongoing bullet-point list at airports sitting against a mauve wall with a raccoon or grizzly bear or some other cartoon animal on a mural behind me.

- She must have felt like she was reinventing herself. But to what end?
- How can she be content with who she's become?
- Has she actually changed, become someone new, or is she just fleeing who she is? Does it matter? Is there a difference?
- Does this new person have any regard for herself, for others, any ability to express herself?
- She's pushed everyone away she cares for, keeping secrets, acting on impulse. What does this say about her?
- How could we have misjudged each other so grossly?
- What does it say about someone who can so quickly and so radically revise themselves?
- Did she ever love me?
- Was he ever in our house?
- Has he touched my cats? He must have been in our house.

I asked Nick if he would dispose of the bottles of alcohol Nina had left on the kitchen counter. I didn't dwell on the lack of consideration, the willful provocation in leaving a cache of alcohol in the house with an alcoholic; it seemed inconsequential given everything else. And to be honest, what disturbed me wasn't the deed itself, but the number of bottles and what they implied. It was a quantity for an intimate holiday gathering, rather than just enough to obliterate one person's troubles. Two bottles of vodka, gin, whiskey. There were too many options. I could have understood a bottle of whiskey half-full, but not the two glasses in the freezer. I knew Richard had been in our apartment.

I asked Nick what I told myself I wouldn't.

"Did you know anything? Did you know this was happening? Tell me."

"I know she saw Richard before she left for Mexico."

I told Nick I needed to go home. We drove in silence. At home, key in the door, my body began to falter and Nick was required to prop me up, wedged against his body and a stucco wall as he opened the door. Inside he laid me down on the couch. He knew I hadn't eaten in days and immediately gave me a glass of water, pulled out the only thing in the refrigerator, Fakin' Bacon, and started to cook. It was over. After all this, she had seen him again. I didn't want to nourish my body in order to stand, to walk, to produce the energy my body required in order to live. Nick hand-fed me like an invalid and I acted like one, refusing to eat the small pieces he had broken up for me. I hadn't been to an AA meeting in years, maybe seven. I checked online to find the times and locations of my neighborhood meetings. I felt like I should know just in case.

January 3, 2007
Dear Richard,

Setting aside my absolute anger and disgust with you as a person, I believe that you, as an educator, must have possessed at some point in your life some understanding of ethics and common decency. It is to the memory of this understanding that I appeal when I ask you to discontinue your relationship and indeed all contact with my wife. Remember for the time being she is still my wife. Perhaps such an appeal is futile when made to someone who has exhibited such selfish, reckless, and gross disregard towards others, and moreover, to one so devoid of sympathy that he has chosen to perpetuate such destructive and hurtful behavior even after its devastating effects on others became well known to him. In the end, I just want you to stay away from her, no matter what principle or strength or fear you have to call upon in order to keep your distance. The damage has been done, and although you are certainly in part responsible for it, if there is any possibility of repair, it must certainly be done without you.

Brett

Richard's response was, for all intents and purposes, a business letter. My letter demanded his letter's composition, and it was composed with the precaution of a lawyer. I understand that there was nothing he could have said. He apologized. There was no response that would have satisfied me, short of: "I fucked up. As I write this my wrists have been cut and are slowly bleeding out."

January 4, 2007
11:35 AM

ME: What time is the marriage counselor?

ME: What does that mean?

ME: Did you listen to what Marty said when we were there last time? He said I could have helped us months ago. That if we weren't both committed to working on this together, there was no point. And in your last comment, were you meaning to hit such a sarcastic tone?

ME: Oh, good, then can I say fuck you?

ME: Pissed at what?

ME: At yourself? I hope.

ME: Not really any reason to be pissed at me.

ME: I don't think a marriage counselor is the answer to anything. He might be able to help if we were working towards something; but, let's face it, you are utterly selfish. You have made up your mind regarding how you feel. It is something YOU need to work on, not us.

ME: You keep using those words but have no insight into what they mean to you, and your choice to not make a choice is a choice and if it is not already very clear to you, here it is: Your choice has devastating results.

ME: You can't do anything to make any of this any easier on me, and now it is transparent you are trying to save face by going to counseling, to be able to say "I gave it the old college try. I tried to work things out, but things have progressed so badly we couldn't." And you know what, at this point, I would hate myself for making any of this easier on you, although on the other hand I also hate myself for suppressing my own impulse to do so, and I resent you for it. Having the choice made for you absolves you of some of the guilt.

ME: I think your confusion is about how you could hurt me or that you don't now want things to go even more badly for me, but these are all thoughts you should have had long ago. And you didn't. And you can't. And you won't.

ME: Oh by the way, I looked at your emails, and there is a new one from Richard waiting there in your junk folder.

ME: You don't seem to have any ability to shed any light on anything, so I thought maybe your emails would.

January 6, 2007
Dear Friends,

Thought I would drop you a line to let you know the marriage is over.

Love,
Brett

January 6, 2007
Marie,

Thank you for your email and your kindness and generosity. You've been an amazing mother-in-law. It sincerely means a lot to me, though it is not surprising since it is how your family has welcomed and treated me from the beginning. I've reached out to a lot of friends who are talking me through the day and I'm sure the days to come. I am flying to NY today for a week and staying with Sam and Evelyn. It is important to me that you are strong through this, especially for Nina. I know she feels devastated and it must be difficult for her to navigate her own feelings, as I know it has been for me. I appreciate everything, but really am not thinking that far in the future yet and really can't process more than a day or so at a time. It goes without saying that I will always be here and that I don't wish to lose you or your family and especially Nina from my life and will make every effort that is emotionally possible. This is just all very devastating for everyone involved, and I wish it had never turned out this way. It is not what I ever wanted. I love Nina dearly and will continue to keep a large place of hope in my heart for her and her happiness whether it is with me or without me.

Love,
Brett

January 16, 2007
Dear Nina,

This is my fundamental problem and how I see things differently than you do: At some point in time, in the not-far-off past, you loved me. We spent five years together happy and in love and made a mutual decision to spend more years together, perhaps have children and build a life with each other. Now, there may be some problems with that statement, emotions that I might be assuming which maybe are incorrect such as "happy" and "love," but I am assuming the best and that you felt that way and were not in a state of confusion, though it is possible you were. This is not to say there weren't problems or issues, but my assumption was that there was a strong foundation of love and a willingness to work through issues as they arose. I watched my parents' divorce and it wasn't something I desired to replicate, and thus didn't enter into this marriage lightly. I knew that life was not easy, that in fact it was tremendously difficult, and I had found a person who I would help through those times and who would help me through those times. I knew that marriage was a long affair and that things would shift and adjust like, how we thought about each other when we were 40, or how things might adjust when we had children. But I held onto the notion of "for better or for worse."

There is no way to reconcile anything. That's certainly what you keep stating and I keep feverishly ignoring. All I can leave California with are uncertainties. To remember and repeat each sentence uttered again and again in my head, to search what little you confessed for larger cracks, to lay the texts before me on an autopsy table to dissect and search for hidden signs. What does it matter that you told your mother "I have met someone else?" Was that easier to say than "I've cheated on Brett?" Does this betray you in some way? What does it mean that you keep telling me "I care about you, I care so much about you," but not "I love you?"

This is all relatively new or at least this rupture—just a month old—but you have been walking around with this feeling in your gut for a year, without providing me the opportunity to question it or work on it with you. Perhaps that time is too long to conquer, but I think I deserve a commitment to work it out, with the knowledge that it might not—but that we would fight for something we thought was valuable. And that is where my disappointment is strongest, because of course I would work on myself and my issues, and to suggest I wouldn't is to miss a large part of who I am, and the things I have done and overcome and dealt with. Life and love go through phases, and we let something drift to the brink, but that doesn't mean we shouldn't try to bring it back. That is what I am asking. To try. And you don't want to, you stand with your blank face, limp arms like someone who is dead, and that is what truly destroys me, since it erases the past and any imagined future. You will be erased.

Brett

A day before *The Phone Call*, the book that Nina and I had just finished editing arrived in the mail. A beautiful hardback of collected readings for wedding ceremonies with a silver dust jacket. It is true sometimes things are as predictable as a bad movie. The book was an anthology of "classic and contemporary prose, poems, excerpts from love letters and novels, and aphorisms" that we had spent the past year working on together. When I was in Minneapolis visiting Noah, the publisher emailed to ask if we would be available to schedule regional radio interviews. *Someday*, I thought, *this will be a funny story*.

2

I packed the three suitcases I owned with clothing and moved back to New York. I was temporarily staying with my friends Jess and Todd in Harlem and halfheartedly searching for my own apartment, stalled in a ditch of post-relationship apathy, depression, and the terror of starting over. I slogged through Craigslist ads: airy, great location, shiny hardwood floors, a window, a counter for a coffeemaker, fits a bed. I wasn't asking for much. I looked at apartments in Midtown, in Inwood, in Brooklyn. Brokers were quick to inform me I didn't earn enough to afford a studio in Manhattan; I should be looking in Queens or the Bronx, which translated as "I'd rather not waste my time on a small commission." Unfamiliar roommates were a distant option, though I came complete with two cats and their unattractive accessories—tumbleweeds of fur and stray litter kicked from a plastic box filled with shit—and my own pathetic baggage of sadness casting shadows across my face. In my early twenties, I had lived in apartments with roaches and small mice visible only by their small pellets on the gas stove. In one apartment, my landlord's cats crawled up in the space between the outer and inner wall and pissed—an oblong damp stain appearing on the ceiling of the apartment and a telltale stench that it was time to move on and out. I was getting too old for that. By chance, a friend emailed me a listing and in the rush to submit my application, I listed my yearly salary as my monthly income. I signed the lease the next day.

I furnished my new apartment in Brooklyn with half the knickknacks Nina and I once owned in Oakland. A shadowbox displaying my wisdom teeth, a painting of a caribou from a childhood friend, a pillow embroidered with the likeness of one of my cats, and an antique print of a Hindu god above my desk. When I left I hadn't wanted to take anything that was ours, the furniture we bought together at the Alameda swap meet, the vintage library desk, a large antique rug, a framed page of a fifteenth-century French breviary with our initials in ornate dropped caps that was a wedding gift from my brother Simon. I didn't want the dishes, the spoons, the forks, or anything else from the registry. I regret leaving my toolbox—a miscellany of screwdrivers, drills, nails, and a hammer—most likely all Christmas gifts from my father, and that realistically I never had occasion to use, but that were unequivocally mine. They were too heavy and impractical to ship, and I wasn't going to ask for anything. I took one pocket-sized tool—a stocking stuffer—a miniature screwdriver set shaped like a football. I left everything I could, every painting or bookcase still firmly there, hooked to a wall so an earthquake couldn't knock it down. Everything felt half full of half empty. I applied a fresh coat of paint to my apartment's bare walls.

Friends called to check in; we talked about what people in their late twenties talk about on the phone—whether we were going to a party at a mutual acquaintance's apartment and whom we would or wouldn't be happy to see there. My friend told me she had just painted the inside of her apartment door gold, in order to reinforce the notion that beyond the entryway the outside world wasn't sepia and slowly rusting. I was fortunate to have a job—my old job in fact, an administrative position at a poetry nonprofit that I'd held before moving to Oakland. I was fortunate my return to the city didn't involve hours sending form letters, waiting in a lobby for an interview, keeping my arms close to my body to avoid exposing possible sweat marks. There was a certain eerie stability in returning to the exact desk where I had already sat for seven years.

When I hung up, I was alone again with my cats—two felines in a small apartment keeping desperate company, fulfilling their duty to be there for me, a cliché and a subtle stay against complete solitude. I never planned it this way. Nothing made sense. The book of my life was suddenly inscrutable. I opened it to look for clues. When I flipped back to the beginning it was as if my entire story had been redacted by some middle-management clerk in an office park in Delaware—he had received orders from the higher-ups to erase the narrative actions and details that had propelled me forward. I needed to create order, to define a narrative, to reach out to someone.

Dear Mom,

As I write this, it is raining; I watch a puddle to confirm that the invisible is happening before my eyes. One pin prick after another. A passing garbage truck shakes the apartment walls. This letter will not reach your mailbox, will not leave my apartment. I swear this isn't a perfunctory assignment from my therapist to uncover a core list of grievances; an attempt to articulate and in so articulating purge all I wish I could or could not say. Nothing is that easy. Where does one begin? There is much which separates us, more than a shadow cast between two unidentified objects measuring the passage of time. There is much I'm unable or unwilling to explain, much that has accumulated and must be discarded in order to move forward.

Where should I begin? I concentrate; sit in the dark with eyes closed. This is how people try to remember things, to attempt to recall the earliest memory available, something like a slug moving down a wall, the blue backdrop, the color of the wall, my body and the edges it created, the air moving in currents against my head. I have no such memories—all that passes through are photographs, an outline requiring shading to become three-dimensional, stories which require me to color in the details, factual or not, based on some thread of history, a perspective from which to view anything. I think: A boy believes his mother loves him, until he doesn't. Then I think: Either the boy was unlovable, or the mother could not love. Somewhere in between there is an antechamber full of doubt where I wait; paintings of Monet's water lilies hang in a gold frame on the wall, I fill out insurance forms. Knowing there is no cure, I resort to paying a professional to talk about it.

The radiator is hissing. I try to recall everything. The dead end, with acres of woods behind our house. It is not a metaphor; it is where we lived, an actual location, a rectangle between two houses, baseball bases painted on the black asphalt. In the woods were a series of tree forts, ditches dug until we reached the tough red clay. Fireflies appeared when the streetlamps flickered on and we swung at the insects with yellow whiffle ball bats.

I remember the Torture Chamber, a "game" Paul and I begged Simon to play. In the middle of the summer months, he held us under heavy covers on his bed—sitting on our legs to prohibit movement, a wadded tissue in our mouth to muffle the squeals, and then, only then, he turned on the blow-dryer and aimed the hot air at our faces. Something in a younger brother wants so much the approval and attention of the older brother, by any means necessary. With Paul I was more an accomplice than victim. He was the mastermind and I was the face of the operation—whether it was a well-worn trick, like betting me I couldn't complete the task of cleaning our room in five minutes or sending me pleading for money for the ice cream truck. He stood lookout at the top of the stairs while I searched your closet for Christmas gifts: a drum set, Sega Genesis, a Walkman.

Mostly I remember that you were sequestered in the master bedroom drinking, watching programs on the black and white television with rabbit ears while your husband and four boys watched football downstairs. I recall curling up in the warmth of your green robe three times the size of a child. Later, you drove me in a blue Toyota to the hospital, my appendix about to rupture. I remember running out of my bedroom in the middle of a late night fight shouting "Stop! Stop!" You were at the bottom of the stairs, my father at the top. You threw a jar of peanut butter at his head. Noah cleaned it up the next morning, like removing chewing gum from hair.

I remember my childhood as a series of fights between you and my father, but the sizes and dimensions of childhood traumas loom disproportionately large in the imagination. According to my brothers, there were only three or four "major" fights. On several occasions you slept in the maroon family van parked in the dead end or left the house in the middle of the night to drive six hours to your mother's house in Virginia.

Eventually you moved to an apartment in a gray town closer to the city, twenty minutes away on the Pennsylvania turnpike. Each school morning you drove from affordable grimness to the house where you once lived, the house you cashed in an inheritance to purchase. Each morning, you arrived after my father had departed for work. You arrived to ensure I made it out the door to wait at the bus stop. Each morning, or so it seemed, your anger with my father found me. I was there standing with my backpack and books to receive every "fuck him" you uttered while reading the lawyer's papers he left out on the counter. Or worse, "He couldn't give a fuck about you; he only wants to fuck me out of money." Some days I'd walk to the bus stop, my hand in the air waving as you drove past on your way to work, then I'd double-back, hiding in the woods, waiting for the bus to arrive and collect my classmates. I waited a few minutes longer and snuck back to the empty house and went to my bedroom to sleep.

Do you remember any of this? You moved back home with a man I barely knew. He did landscaping at the Red Roof Inn. One night, he fell asleep drunk and naked on the pull-out couch in the living room. It was clear it wasn't my father's house anymore. Or do you remember how you gripped Simon's arm with desperation when he threatened to throw a six pack of Genesis Ale out the back door into the woods? It was dusk, a strange light still half-visible over the horizon, part shadow, part truth. A few weeks later, in July 1992, I wrote in my journal: "I slept over at my father's house. We played tennis. I am pretty good. My dad hurt his ankle really bad (he's on crutches now). The next day we went birthday shopping. I got three pairs of jeans, three hooded shirts, two cassette tapes. I still have my mom's birthday money too. That evening my mom got a case of beer. She was really drunk by 7:00. There was a huge argument. And she told me and my brothers to leave. I have to learn to keep my cool with the drunk and not to let her get to me. It's really hard. Simon, who hardly ever yells at her, was yelling last night (Noah too)."

It was the first time in years, with Simon and Noah home from college for the summer, that you would have all four sons under one roof. It was a month before I entered the eighth grade, two weeks before my thirteenth birthday, when in a drunken outburst you told me to leave. When I packed the last of my things, I stole your boyfriend's John Lennon records and his copy of *The Catcher in the Rye*. In my journal I noted: "We went by the old house to get a few things. My mother called that night. She told my dad that if I entered the house when she wasn't there, she would call the police."

Love,
Brett

After living in my new apartment for two months, I had begun to settle into starting over. A new combination of medications had, for the time being, brought a halt to tearful situations with friends recounting and questioning my failed marriage on the subway or in the booth of an empty diner at a late hour. In general my anxiety was mild enough to allow me to depart my apartment, out three consecutive doors onto the street to purchase coffee, and then back to my apartment. Grind more beans. Drink the pot black. Pace, and return to the computer screen.

I was slowly beginning to feel a part of my new neighborhood, had established routines: a favorite takeout restaurant, a coffee shop that played loud 90s punk music and gave me a frequent customer punch card, and a bodega where the man behind the counter reached for my brand of cigarettes as I opened the door. I began to recognize my block's regulars, mostly twitching meth addicts who bummed cigarettes from me in front of an aid building. There was a semi-homeless woman, who stepped out in front of me one evening as I stood at the crosswalk waiting for the light to change. She gingerly pulled her skirt up to expose her genitalia while staring directly at me, and let out the smallest tinkle of urine down her leg. Afterwards she asked for a light and kept her gaze on me as I lit her cigarette. "I saw you lookin'," she said.

There were the various men who stood against the metal gate to my apartment door selling porn DVDs and loosies. We would exchange nods and they would call out "How you livin', David Spade?" I assumed they had nicknamed me after the actor because I, too, was short and blond, but that was the extent of the similarity I allowed. (Sometimes when I had facial stubble they would call me Steven Spielberg.) These men always came to my assistance. When I was locked out, one of the gentlemen produced a screwdriver from his waistband to jimmy the lock. When a single pallet of seventy boxes from Oakland was delivered and left on the sidewalk in front of the liquor store in my building, one of the men offered to make sure nothing happened to them for ten bucks. I carried the boxes, mostly books, two at a time up the two flights and stacked them three feet high against a Harbor Fog–painted wall. One of these same men punched me in the face after I told him I didn't have any spare change, but the next morning upon exiting my apartment he was there with hand outstretched and an apology: "I think I knocked someone's glasses off last night." I'd lived in Brooklyn off and on for ten years, so I knew statistically I had it coming. I accepted his apology. I knew this neighborhood and there was nothing I would fear here. I felt welcomed home.

And by "home," I mean nothing more than a set of characteristics I had grown comfortable with. I preferred the verticalness of New York to the suburban sprawl of the Bay Area, a place without personal history for me and populated with people who made small talk too quickly and with too much ease. I preferred the day trip to Coney Island to eat a hot dog and watch the barges of trash gradually move across the ocean's horizon to a hike through ancient redwoods. The cars of California were everywhere. It was clear you couldn't make it there without a hatchback and reasonable gas mileage.

I knew I was a creature of habit, knew my city's quirks and had grown accustomed to them: how to jaywalk with a sense of impunity; that it took ten seconds to cross an avenue as the crosswalk timer counted down, but I could do it in four seconds if required; how long my eyes could linger on a stranger; or that as I waited for a friend in a café she would be either ten minutes early or ten minutes late depending on the trains. I first arrived in New York in 1998 to live with my college girlfriend. She was studying painting, and I arrived to become a poet. It was my city, and I was in love with it before I was in love with Nina. It was sentimental. It was a chip on my shoulder, like how I can speak ill of a family member and jump to their defense at the first disparaging remark from a non-family member. It was the city where I lost eighty dollars playing Three-card Monte, and the city where I attended my first poetry reading by poets whose books I had read. It was family, and its shortcomings were all mine now. My brief stint in another city, Pittsburgh, felt like a detour in a small town, until I accepted the burden of exorbitant loans—which only the wild-eyed stargazer would find wise—to transfer to a school in New York City.

I know these sentiments read like a starry-eyed love letter—distance makes the heart grow fonder, or stronger, or wronger. But having been so long absent from the city it became my estranged lover, and I was filled with anguish, like the lover who needs to see his beloved who is holed up somewhere in a hotel in a faraway city on a work trip, who is down the street, or at work. Back in New York, I thought of the year and a half I was not here and of a letter John Keats wrote to his lover Fanny Brawne:

> I cannot exist without you—I am forgetful of every thing but seeing you again—my Life seems to stop there—I see no fur-ther. You have absorb'd me. I have a sensation at the present moment as though I was dissolving—I should be exquisitely miserable without the hope of soon seeing you. I should be afraid to separate myself far from you.

I had sent a slightly less eloquent email to my friend Francesca in my first month in California when Nina and I were staying with friends in Occidental while we searched for an apartment in Oakland:

> Blah, blah, blah. Do you want to hear about my day trips and the weather? Should I tell you about the sheep and the amazing garden here on the property where I eat fresh car-rots and peas and beans? Aren't you just frustrated with curi-osity? This morning I woke up and asked Nina if we could go home now. We can't. And though it is super-relaxing up here in the country, it is beginning to get more and more difficult to believe that I will be living out on this coast in a stucco house. I don't know what I am supposed to do but deal with it and get

all mellow and dig the fresh air. Yesterday I heard someone say "hella" and they weren't kidding. This is how it goes.

Around the time I returned to New York from California, an excerpt of E. B. White's famous essay "Here is New York" was posted in the subway system as part of a public arts program. It was the section in which he distinguished between three types of New Yorkers: those who were actually born here; the commuters; and those, like me, who arrived from elsewhere with an idealized vision of the city. It is that final category of New Yorkers to whom he ascribes the city's "poetical deportment." We had arrived in the capital of commerce, the land of the wishful profiteers and poets, with romantic dreams of becoming someone or something, and if not, then to have the comfort of becoming anonymous.

April 1, 2007
N.,

I'm perplexed at your insistence that I refrain from anger in my emails to you; by your reasoning anger is not "constructive" and not helpful to coordinating whatever it is we have left to coordinate. This feels entirely disingenuous to me that you could pretend to be taking the high road, to suddenly be retreating to the language of therapy and self-help. Is this some strategy your therapist advised? Maybe she could have also suggested coming clean months ago, when for so long you were unable to address any of this in any productive or healthy fashion. Does my anger make you think less of me as a person? How much less could you possibly think? It's funny, since I think, in general, except for spitting at you, which was disgraceful and I'm embarrassed and sorry for, I have acted very compassionately and sympathetic to you, talking with honesty and candor about how I felt and what I thought without resorting to real name calling or destructive actions, which I think many others would have. I'm angry, and personally I think you should experience this anger and disappointment. This isn't the type of anger I will burn through in a week. In fact, I'm sure the self-help literature would suggest I express my anger rather than keep it subdued and shelved. Your constant insincere insistence of "I know you are angry" only attempts to minimize my expression of hurt, while portraying it as somehow invalid and irrational. I'm angry; do you expect me not to be? What do you expect from me? Do you imagine I could be wholly sympathetic to your position which intrinsically alienates me, or rather, how should I put it? Fucks Me Over? Do you truly think you are in any position to be talking about hurtful behavior? And though you say you wouldn't talk that way to me, well, I wouldn't cheat on you as a symptom of my frustration towards you or my relationship with you and then, get this, continue and continue to do it after it has been exposed, denied, downplayed. Your hands are dirty, and I know you must now have them full with working out how to forgive yourself.

As to pushing you away, how much further could I possibly push you away? Where to? Our relationship is clearly over. Destroyed. In your most recent email, you note casually our lack of intimacy started before any of this. Of course it started before this. But I have to say that your responsibility looms larger in my mind than mine. It was always your inability, your spurning my advances, your uncomfortable-ness with me and not vice-versa. You cooled on me. I recall numerous occasions asking if something was wrong, and it was always explained as your inability to share such a degree of intense closeness with anyone, so much so you told me you believed it would be easier to have sex with a stranger than with me. I remember asking you, even back when we lived in New York, if you loved me more like a brother.

But it wasn't working, and when something doesn't work, junk it. I will accept my failures. You're right, this was a relationship and I'm also responsible for my participation or nonparticipation which led to its failure, and though I would love to point fingers (and I'm pretty sure in what direction I would point them) I will accept my failures, which according to you include a neediness and anxiety, both of which I have experienced in varying degrees and imagine I will feel for the rest of my life, just as I believe you will deal with varying degrees of depression and anxiety at future points in your life. The only time you honestly addressed these concerns to me was the time you told me you stayed at work late because you didn't want to come home to someone so unhappy; I immediately went to the doctor and started taking anti-depressants. And the other time, when you said you would like to go to therapy together, I told you I "had no problem with that" which you took as a sarcastic or dismissive comment and never followed up. I know I could have also followed up on this, but I was shut down in my depression. I was alone in the apartment working while you were at work; I couldn't drive myself anywhere, and didn't know where to go if I'd had my license. I hadn't made many friends at graduate school, and missed New York, the city itself, the connection to my friends and a group of other writers. I could have shown some incentive. Rode the bus somewhere. But it was a vicious cycle: knowing I needed to find a group of people to interact with and yet being too depressed to motivate myself to make the effort.

You are right that depression is part of me, something I need to work on and be aware of. And it is important that both of us find a partner who can deal with the other's depression. You cast my depression in comparison to yours, to which you reacted proactively and with strength to work through it. You're right, you did, and it was impressive and I will never take that away from you. However, I would like to point out that you had a base of support to come home to, to call up on the phone and talk you through it when your strength failed you. This is something I didn't have or couldn't reach out for and it only created more resentment in you towards me. Your strength was amazingly found within you but was also fostered by those that loved you. Perhaps you overlooked my depression since it was not as outwardly tearful as yours, but a numbness which made it difficult for me to reach out, especially when I felt like there was no one to reach out to. Remember me telling you I wasn't even able to email my friends, to keep in touch with them about the most mundane everyday things? Surely that must have hinted at something much more than mere unhappiness. You seem to even resent it, that I wasn't proactive, that you had to nudge me towards help. I want to point out that is what partners do.

And you're right to suggest that it is only between you and me, and not the heartthrob you fell in love with and fucked only to come home to me and order takeout and watch *Law & Order*. Maybe I would be willing to place that in a cavern in my mind and hope that it disappeared over time, but it is still present in your willingness to seek out comfort in this person, even when you know it is destructive to someone you "care so much about." You wouldn't even make a provisional commitment to not see him, email him, or date him, and looked at me incredulously when I suggested you shouldn't continue to work there with him. If it was just about us, then shouldn't he have been out of the picture for at least the time we were trying to figure things out?

Clearly not,
B.

Most evenings, in Brooklyn, on arriving home from work, I smoked a thousand cigarettes and indiscriminately and illegally downloaded *Pitchfork*'s recommended albums by New England trust fund kids with asymmetrical haircuts who noodled away with effects pedals and keyboards, transforming bleeps and beats into patterns, or the newest hip-hop sensation from Ghana. It kept me feeling informed and, if called upon, able to participate in the conversation my demographic was having at the coffee shop. More importantly, I discovered the benefit of devising purposeless tasks to occupy and account for my leisure hours. I set time aside to reorder my Netflix queue, to curate a rotation of films with enough variety to anticipate the mixture of possible moods and minimize the potential that the rectangular red envelope remained unopened in a stack of junk mail and bills. I organized the list so that on any given occasion my selections consisted of a documentary, a romantic comedy, and a foreign or classic film: *The Bridge*, *Juno*, or *The Night of the Hunter*.

Some nights I would fall asleep on the hardwood floor, the back of my shoulders propped against the couch, a book folded open and resting on my chest. As I would come to the end of a sentence, the logic of its grammar would vanish and I would drift into the subject matter of dreams. Living alone with no supervision, I'd reverted to a childlike indifference to proper conduct, and with no parent or partner to wake me; I slept where I placed myself. In a small apartment, surrounded by all my belongings, nothing had been right for a long time and there was no one, except for myself, to remove me.

Once every two weeks I received an email from Nina. A UPS tracking number, a request for confirmation of receipt of legal documents, notice that The National were playing in Brooklyn, questions regarding the well-being of my cats, inquiries if I was receiving her emails, which I was no longer responding to, confirmation that she received legal documents.

Other nights on the floor, I watched the ceiling fan spin a continuous gray shadow while I contemplated the practical minutiae surrounding the single person's universal dilemma: dying alone and unnoted in their apartment. The archetypal slip in the shower. A gas leak. Heart failure. I calculated the probable amount of time that would pass before my body would be found. I liked to think of it as a version of Sudoku. Each factor placed in the scenario altered the course of events. *If I die tonight. If I die this weekend. If I die on a holiday weekend—I will grow cold. It would be a Wednesday night when, prompted by my work colleagues, my landlord knocks on the door; an eerie silence lingers, a locksmith is called. I'm not going anywhere. I should give a friend a set of spare keys.*

The fan kept spinning and my mind moved elsewhere, revisiting and taking inventory of every injustice perpetrated against me. When I'd exhausted childhood traumas, my teenage years, and my marriage, I started cataloging recent insults, friends who hadn't returned my emails from the day before. Even as I recognized the pointless destructiveness of such trains of thought, I couldn't stop. Instead, acknowledging my self-loathing sent me wandering further down dark corridors until I was standing on the welcome mat to rooms with more advanced torture devices, including the coup de grace: suicide.

I placed a Post-It note on my bathroom mirror that read "It will get better." I repeated over and over: "It is getting better." A book on cognitive approaches to healthy living suggested that I do something like this, that if we change the dead-end paths our thoughts follow, we are on a road to somewhere else. These books were filled with such insights. There were volumes to read, and so little to learn. Or maybe there was nothing to learn and the point was to have an objective third party state the obvious. I wanted to believe I was becoming a better, more self-aware person with each chapter, with each analogy I encountered in the vast body of self-help literature—the type of books that might posit men are from New Jersey and women are from New Mexico, books with titles like *Dang, Dude! You're Getting a Divorce* that your father might give you to navigate the emotional pain. Books that would contextualize my suffering with something like "The Parable of The Rusted Nail."

You are walking carefree through the autumn foliage on a weekend apple-picking trip. Close your eyes to picture this if it helps. You are walking on a crisp day; your thoughts are elsewhere, maybe on the game. Imagine the weight of the Golden Delicious apples you are carrying in a wicker basket. Really feel that weight in your arms. Close your eyes and begin to catalog all the apples you have ever known: Fuji, Gala, Granny Smith, Gravenstein, McIntosh. If you are a sensitive type perhaps imagine you were contemplating lines from a poem memorized in a high school English class: "But I was well / Upon my way to sleep before it fell, / And I could tell / What form my dreaming was about to take." Suffice it to say, you are preoccupied with your thoughts, as you often were in your relationship, only half-listening, with your eyes on the road or on the television. You are observing the clear blue sky, one foot in front of the other on the brown grass, not paying full attention to the path you are treading, and then it happens. You lift your left leg and place your foot down on a rusted nail in a discarded piece of wood, maybe from an old barn or picket fence. It will come as a painful shock. The nail pierces the worn sole of your tennis shoe, damp from the morning dew. Your partner says, "I need some time and space to think about our relationship." You are a man, so there are two options. You stoically ignore it, or you let slip the phrase "Fuck my world!" and try to take a few brave steps forward as pain travels slowly up your leg. You might hold back the tears, until, on further investigation of the wound, you notice the blood. At the sight of blood your eyes water, or maybe you feel faint. The point is that the pain will subside. You go to the hospital and get a shot. You walk tenderly for a month, perhaps a year, but after time your strut will return. In a few months, you might think: I should have known something like that would happen; it really was too cold out there for apple-picking.

I took *Othello* down from my bookshelf. Misguided, jealous, tragically flawed or not, I felt, *Finally, here is someone who gets me.* "O curse of marriage, / That we can call these delicate creatures ours, / And not their appetites! I had rather be a toad, / And live upon the vapor of a dungeon, / Than keep a corner in the thing I love / For others' uses." Even knowing the misfortune on the horizon, this meant more to me. I put out the light and went to sleep.

One night I settled on watching *The Bridge*, a documentary about "the mythic beauty of the Golden Gate Bridge, the most popular suicide destination in the world, and those drawn by its call." There was a woman in the documentary paralyzed with grief from her friend's 245-foot plunge. She was understandably unable to bring herself to drive across the bridge. The bridge was ruined for her. The bridge is ruined, each year, hundreds of times. Each time, in fog or sunlight, no matter what season and how grandiose the beauty of the structure, it holds up that memory. One young man interviewed had managed to survive his suicidal leap into the cold Pacific. There is a poem written by Ted Berrigan and Anne Waldman that in part recounts a similar story:

> I asked Tuli Kupferberg once, "Did you really jump off of The Manhattan Bridge?" "Yeah," he said, "I really did." "How come?" I said. "I thought that I had lost the ability to love," Tuli said. "So, I figured I might as well be dead. So, I went one night to the top of The Manhattan Bridge, after a few minutes, I jumped off." "That's amazing," I said. "Yeah," Tuli said, "but nothing happened. I landed in the water, & I wasn't dead. So I swam ashore, & went home, & took a bath, & went to bed. Nobody even noticed."

I abandoned the possibility of jumping from a bridge as a viable option. Self-inflicted death should be foolproof, or else one is forced to continue life with an additional failure. It isn't so much that I thought about suicide, but a substantial rest from an interior life. The profound advantage of being done. I thought, *It's possible that "one day at a time" leads to a life lived.* I smoked. I didn't want to ruin anything. The world didn't change. There it was again, always there, a lump in my throat, too awkward in shape to swallow, partially obstructing my breath. It was easier to shuffle from bed to kitchen for a glass of water and back to bed than to open the front door to what was on the street below.

There were times I thought I hadn't taken my own life not from fear, but from utter laziness. The work involved in figuring it out was exhausting. The easiest and most efficient method was to order pills from Canada, which may or may not be the item advertised. The blue sugar pills would sail through my veins in vain. How embarrassing to vomit up a bottle of aspirin or placebos as the body rejects the mind's wishes. I looked around my apartment for a beam that could bear the load. Therapists only take a suicidal client seriously if she or he has a plan. I wanted to be taken seriously. It was with more than morbid curiosity that I found myself following my thought experiments to their conclusions. It was a familiar pattern, off and on since childhood, in which the imagined events became confused with reality until I began to wonder if I'd already completed the act and was a walking ghost. Alone, with no immediate prospects to end the solitude, I thought: *Regarding suicide, nothing is extraordinary. To take action in one's own death isn't cowardly. It might be cowardly to remain.*

I remained cowardly. My brain traveled the familiar neural pathways that my past history of depression had worn, and my brain recalled the previous methods I utilized to deal with or forget my depression. I mean to say my gray matter is a solid hue of gray, devoid of hints of color, leaning neither towards a brighter shade of hopeful white nor the depraved black of nothingness. My gray is a perpetual cloudy day. The two most radical ways I had previously attempted to change this palette were 1) praying to the blue god Krishna or 2) drinking until I passed out, and both were options I had forgone long ago. Still, almost weekly, I checked online for the schedule of services at the Brooklyn Hare Krishna Temple and the times of the local AA meetings.

In my childhood household, alcohol served the purpose of faith—that is, it provided a coping mechanism for the inevitable death lurking in all of us. My parents' routine screaming matches traveled at light speed towards divorce, and then there was the viciousness, the pettiness, and the sadness of the divorce itself. Experts report that during such spells of emotional vulnerability, individuals are susceptible to new religions, cults, and utopian societies. After the death of a loved one, a tragedy, or an upheaval of their daily routine, they may find themselves waiting for a sign, like the lunar eclipse marking the messianic end or heaven's gates creaking open. The *Bhagavad Gita* explains that there are "four types of pious person that render devotional service unto Krishna; the distressed, the seeker of knowledge, desirers of wealth, and men of wisdom." If I'm being generous I was two or three of these—but I was unequivocally distressed. I had a distinct feeling that at any moment, my family, my whole world, might just cave in. The tectonic faults and vibrations were just below the surface and at any moment they could rupture. There was no identifiable "earthquake weather"; certain cloud formations on a calm day are as dangerous as certain cloud formations on any other day. The needle rested until it tremored unexpectedly, and I knew it was only a matter of time before the earth would open up to swallow me.

It all happened quickly. I was thirteen years old when I began praying to Krishna: a blue boy playing a flute to a herd of sheep on a green hill, a small boy with a peacock feather in his hair and beads around his neck, lotus in bloom almost everywhere around him. I burned incense and chanted the holy name, waiting for a mystical presence to make itself known to me, for a sphere of light to radiate from my fingertips. I began praying before I understood anything about the teachings of Krishna. I only knew it was incumbent to close my bedroom door, turn off the lights, and seek protection from the world. It happened quickly. I was young. There was little opportunity for a family intervention. I simply came home one night with a shaved head. The difference between the three-inch mohawk I had when I left for school and the ponytail tuft on the crown of my head when I returned must have seemed to my father a question of semantics.

I found ways to occupy my time. I made a suicide to-do list. It's important to delete computer files, history, cookies. My last site visited shouldn't be Cute Overload, Craigslist Missed Connections, or worse. When my computer arrived from Oakland, I plugged in my iPod. Twenty thousand songs were organized by date added, and the last one, by Beyoncé, had been downloaded by Nina. All Music Guide describes Beyoncé's music as "celebratory, good natured, and uncompromising," and the song "Irreplaceable" is no exception. I watched the video on YouTube, in which Beyoncé portrays a character who refuses to shed a tear for her ex-lover. She indifferently files her nails as the cheater walks out of their apartment with boxes of his belongings. The song is an anthem, empowering the singer to realize she "could have another you in a minute." My ex-wife listened to the song on my computer exactly twenty-four times. I placed the song on repeat and spent too much time contemplating the lyrics. I wanted to ask Beyoncé why, if her lover wasn't special, she bothered with the relationship in the first place.

I began to systematically delete all my photographs of Nina, including any photographs taken by her or suggestive of her presence. Our honeymoon to Dublin, Prague, and Paris went into the trash. I deleted the photos she took of me sitting at a café table with an espresso and a pink macaroon, me in a sombrero with a docile donkey in a port town of Mexico, me posed in front of mating sea lions from our picturesque drive down the Pacific Coast Highway that couples are required to take. All into the trash. I could still see her; almost feel her there on the opposite side of the lens framing me, asserting her existence. She was capturing my image under the false pretense of creating memories we could, at a click of the mouse, recall. The computer prompt asked "Are you sure you want to delete the 253 files?" How quickly they all disappeared, all the quirks and memories effacing themselves.

I should start at the real beginning. In the third century BC, somewhere in Northern India near the border of present day Nepal, Krishna, the Supreme Being, an incarnation of Vishnu, was born. As a young boy he played in the woods, protected the villagers, dodged assassination attempts, lifted a mountain, killed demons, and eventually found himself on an epic battlefield. Refusing to fight, he was a charioteer to Arjuna, the greatest warrior on earth, with whom he discoursed on a variety of topics including mediation and yoga, devotional service, and the nature of material existence. It is this conversation that would become the *Bhagavad Gita*, the sacred text for the Krishna movement.

Five thousand years later, in 1965, the American beginning was marked when, on a religious mission to bring Krishna to America, His Divine Grace A.C. Bhaktivedanta Swami Prabhupada arrived on the Lower East Side of New York City. A year later he established the International Society of Krishna Consciousness, which describes the tenets of Krishna Consciousness in its current media kit as follows:

> People are not their material bodies, but are eternal spirit souls. . . . To achieve Krishna Consciousness effectively, members chant and meditate upon the holy names of Lord Krishna. . . . Members also practice four "principles of religion": compassion, truthfulness, cleanliness, and austerity. . . . They are strict vegetarians, not eating any meat, fish, or eggs. They also abstain from gambling and illicit sex, and do not smoke, drink, or take drugs.

Or maybe we should start at my beginning, 1978, the year of my birth. I wasn't baptized. The truth is, until my adult years, I'd only been inside a church twice. Once when I was seven for a cousin's wedding, and once more when I was eleven. It was the morning after a sleepover at a friend's house. His grandmother dropped us off in front of St. Joseph the Worker in Levittown, Pennsylvania, a town, according to the *Saturday Evening Post*, where "Everybody lives on the same side of the tracks. They have no slums to fret about, no families of conspicuous wealth to envy, no traditional upper crust to whet and thwart their social aspirations." In other words, a community in which everything was going to be okay. Jesus looked down, surrounded by Klee-like geometric stained glass in blue shades, from the main entranceway. I followed my friend down the red-carpeted aisle to the first row of pews. We paused at the empty seats, walked out the side door, and went to the mini-mart to steal cigarettes.

In America, Krishna caught on quickly, or at least the chanting part did. Two years after the arrival of Prabhupada, the poet Allen Ginsberg was singing *Hare Krishna Hare Krishna Krishna Krishna Hare Hare Hare Rama Hare Rama Rama Rama Hare Hare* and playing his harmonium at Vietnam protests. Peace. Love. Freedom. Happiness. The religion received a shout-out of sorts in *Hair: The American Tribal Love-Rock Musical*. And in 1970, George Harrison was topping the charts singing about the Sweet Lord. It was a decade later in the movie *Airplane!*, that Krishna Consciousness was solidified as material for parody:

The Krishnas are approached by the Religious Zealot.

ZEALOT #2: Hello, we'd like you to have this flower from the Church of Consciousness. Would you like to make a donation?

KRISHNA: (shakes his head) No, we gave at the office.

I realized that if I did decide to go through with killing myself, all traces should be wiped clean. Instead of just clearing my browser history, I would remove my hard drive altogether, hammer a nail through it and submerge it in a bowl of rubbing alcohol. Municipal strangers with walkie-talkies would track dirt on my wood floors. I spent an unhealthy amount of time scrubbing those floors. There was little else to do. One of my brothers would be contacted by the authorities. Contagions and rot might hang in the air. The floor would need to be scrubbed with lemon disinfectant, to remove my blood, vomit, and shit. I'd need to leave cleanser out beside the kitchen sink and extra bowls of food for the cats.

To leave the business of sorting and disposing of the debris of a life to someone else might be too cruel. My belongings would be a window one couldn't help put peep into, to search for answers to how and why. What book was on the bedside table? There were volumes of poetry, the *I Ching*, and Cioran's *On the Heights of Despair*, in which this passage would be found underlined: "Is there anything on earth which cannot be doubted except death, the only certainty in this world? To doubt and yet to live—this is a paradox, though not a tragic one, since doubt is less intense, less consuming, than despair."

I concluded one shouldn't die amongst one's things. I thought of taking a cab to one of the airport hotels miles from the city's center. No one would ask questions. If they did, I was a sales rep, I was heading home for the funeral of a distant uncle, on a layover from Houston, from Pittsburgh. I thought: *Let housekeeping find me with my passport on the dresser.* I made lists, noting that each gift I'd been given would be returned to the giver, collections dispersed: a ceramic swallow, a wooden sparrow, a painting of two finches, the photograph of birds on telephone wires, Francis the upholstered swan. Each bird would be given a new home to haunt. It felt no different than packing to move to another city, another borough, just down the street. Each box would be labeled with a person's name. *Fragile. This side up.* The sadness I imagined was someone else's, never my own. Memories would exist in their daily routines, and then months pass and soon a talisman of mine would gather dust in their apartment or be sold at a stoop sale in five years with their Linda Ronstadt records, travel guides, and chipped ceramics.

At thirteen I began the process of renunciation by becoming "straight-edge." *Don't drink, don't smoke, don't fuck.* It was a rigid motto to prop me up. I had fellow straight-edge friends, most of whom I had grown up with or knew from school because we dressed the same, skated the same empty municipal parks, listened to the same music, and were filled with a similar suburban ennui. We acted out; found ourselves in crowded basements and garages, at fire halls with cheap speakers and guitar fuzz. We banged up against others dancing with anger, listened to hardcore music and shouted *Don't drink, don't smoke, don't fuck.* Minor Threat. Chain of Strength. Burn. We marked the backs of our hands with thick black x's that wouldn't wash off for weeks.

In 1992, at a small hardcore club in Center City, Philadelphia, the lead singer of the band Youth of Today was headlining with his new band, Shelter. Teenagers with shaved heads wearing concert tees, chain wallets, baggy jeans, and messenger bags were throwing themselves against one another, against anything, on the checkered dance floor. I sang along: *Security. How secure are we? Making our plans in a castle of sand as our dreams get dragged to sea.* This was the first band of a new movement: Krishnacore.

There are those who, if approached at the right time and place, will convert to anything; perhaps, sadly, I was one of them. And, further, it is reported, these individuals will often experience a "relief effect," a decrease in levels of stress and anxiety. That seems reasonable enough. I find it is important to note that I wasn't alone. There were a dozen or so of us in my high school and we walked the hallways with shaved heads, wearing white undershirts dyed saffron. Our classmates called us the Krishna Mob. In the large cafeteria we bowed our heads over our ice cream sandwiches and chanted a Sanskrit offering to Krishna. I wore the saffron robes to attend my girlfriend's school dance, and then refused to dance with her. I would only dance at the temple or down a crowded street selling books and roses. It was important others see me in this way, that the inner transformation was marked with an outer transformation.

At home, I offered Krishna a freshly washed apple. In the corner of my bedroom, I constructed a makeshift altar: a milk crate covered in a multicolored Mexican blanket, a wooden figurine of Jagannatha (the round-eyed god seen on SMILE stickers sold by Krishnas), a jar of sacred sand from Vrindavan (the forest of Krishna's childhood), a small bronze vase with fresh flowers, and an image of Krishna clipped from the temple newsletter. There were times I kept my right hand clean and my left dirty and did not wear the pendant of Narasimhavatar into the lavatory. I hung the pendant on the doorknob outside the bathroom because such devotional items should not enter unclean spaces. After much adjustment and difficulty I learned to wipe with my left hand. The right hand should remain clean. Eat with the right hand. I looked in a mirror to apply tilak, a chalky sandalwood paste, to the middle of the forehead. Some say the space between the two eyebrows is a sacred spot where the third eye—the sixth chakra, Shiva's eye—appears. Some say the tilak has a cooling effect to aid concentration during meditation. Some say the mark is meant as a sacred distinction, identifying you publicly from nonbelievers.

There were times I refused my body its wishes. Times I gave in to my wishes. Times I turned the wooden figurine towards the wall, as if an all-knowing deity didn't have eyes in the back of his head. Times I could not pinpoint my wishes so I chanted a round: *Hare Krishna Hare Krishna Krishna Krishna Hare Hare Hare Rama Hare Rama Rama Rama Hare Hare.*

My father asked me very little about the religion, but I think he was happy to know my teenage acting out didn't yet involve drugs and alcohol. I was home on time and calling to check in at regular intervals; that, it seemed, was enough. I closed my bedroom door when I burned incense, and though we didn't eat our meals together he purchased microwavable vegetarian meals for me. I placed a small plate of the reheated rice and green peas in front of a wooden icon of Jagannatha, prayed, added the offering back to the larger plate, and ate.

My father did draw the line at my spending the night at the temple, but on Sundays I was permitted to attend the free weekend feast and lecture. It was an hour and a half trip. I took a southern commuter train from suburbia and transferred at the Center City transit hub. Families from around the tri-state area attended the free feast. The gravel parking lot filled up with lawyers, businessmen in khakis, people who worked retail jobs, people who most likely had savings in their bank accounts, hippies with tie-dyed shirts, some people with shaved heads, some people without, some people with kids, numerous Indian families with women in saris, and a few homeless men. All were welcome, all variety of shoes and sandals were left in the main hall. It felt more like a potluck for a progressive school than a religious gathering.

I prayed to God cross-legged on a beige carpet in my father's condominium with jasmine incense burning, waiting for thunder to release from my heart. Night after night with the lights out I chanted before sleep, but morning arrived like any other day, a disruption to my dreams of being elsewhere, of being transported to another life. I had inherited a household absent of religious practices and iconography. There was no cross above the doorway. No holidays for which we were corralled into the station wagon for midnight mass. I looked to the mystical heavens for answers in an attempt to make sense of life, to find an alternative solution in which I was not the only person I could depend on.

I drew lines of comparison. I'd read a Joseph Campbell book or two and created my own personal visualization of all belief systems as a giant rope. Along the rope large knots were tied at equal distance, each one representing a distinctive tradition. I linked chanting the mantra with the garland of roses, linked 108 prayer beads to the fifty beads of the Catholic rosary; linked the act of offering food to Krishna to the Christian "grace," linked a life of celibacy to monks in monasteries in Belgium and nuns in convents in Ireland; and linked the dietary restrictions and vegetarianism to my Jewish neighbors who kept kosher. The four regulative principles of Krishna Consciousness seemed less and less weird: No gambling. No illicit sex (or rather, sex was meant solely for procreation). No intoxicants. No meat, fish, or eggs. I was embarking on a life of purity. A round of chanting takes ten minutes. It is important to keep count, to surrender to the process. Devotees chant sixteen rounds daily. Sixteen rounds takes almost three hours. Three hours of service to the lord took less time than watching a James Cameron movie.

I wanted to believe there was only the moment before I was conscious of Krishna and the moment after. As is often the case, nothing lasted for long. One possible solution to the suffering of *maya*, or illusion, was replaced by another. It all happened quickly. The initial feeling wore off. I could chant the Maha Mantra ad nauseum and the world felt the same. The words I began chanting in 1992 lost meaning. When one door failed to open, I went looking for another exit. I started drinking in 1993.

I watched the fan spin. It had a job to do and did it. I lay in bed and visualized my body as a corpse painted a hue to match my living paleness. I imagined rain falling on the damp earth and the cemetery grass shining with a healthy greenness, nourished by the organic chemicals of the lives below its surface. I had selected the poem to be read at my grave: "Afterwards," by Thomas Hardy.

When the Present has latched its postern behind my
    tremulous stay,
And the May month flaps its glad green leaves like wings,
Delicate-filmed as new-spun silk, will the neighbours say,
"He was a man who used to notice such things"?

If it be in the dusk when, like an eyelid's soundless blink,
The dewfall-hawk comes crossing the shades to alight
Upon the wind-warped upland thorn, a gazer may think,
"To him this must have been a familiar sight."

If I pass during some nocturnal blackness, mothy and warm,
When the hedgehog travels furtively over the lawn,
One may say, "He strove that such innocent creatures should
    come to no harm,
But he could do little for them; and now he is gone."

If, when hearing that I have been stilled at last, they stand at
    the door,
Watching the full-starred heavens that winter sees,
Will this thought rise on those who will meet my face
    no more,
"He was one who had an eye for such mysteries"?

• • •

And will any say when my bell of quittance is heard in
   the gloom,
And a crossing breeze cuts a pause in its outrollings,
Till they rise again, as they were a new bell's boom,
"He hears it not now, but used to notice such things"?

Nothing was happening. I spent my days uninterested in the days that were happening—repetition, which is some version of living, was the dominant mode. I imagined the GPS data from my cell phone visualized as a map—the same route to and from work, the digital lines traced over and over with no variation. And then one night, in bed waiting for sleep to arrive, something did happen. A human-shaped shadow appeared before my bookcases. My cats sensed little or did not perceive a threat. The building I lived in was nondescript. It lacked the character ascribed to haunted sites (i.e. a rambling Victorian in disrepair set apart from the street, shuttered windows and antique furniture covered in white sheets). And yet, something did appear.

On television ghost-hunting shows, a dog will refuse to enter an attic and bark wildly until historic walls are dampened with holy water. Until sage is burned. My cats rested comma-like in the curve of my arm, eyes closed. On television the host announces, "If there is a spirit in the room make yourself known." And then a knock is heard from a location off-camera, the house creaks, a jar filled with sacred sand from India slips from the bookshelf and shatters. A bird—most likely the foreboding raven—caws outside the window. Someone off-camera whispers: "Did you feel that sudden chill?"

I followed the advice I'd gathered from such shows. I spoke to the empty room: "If there is a spirit in the room make yourself known." The next day I bought sage and burned it. Nevertheless, the figure returned that evening. In bed I thought: *It can do me no harm I can't do to myself.* I looked at it from the corner of my eye. Both intimate and unidentifiable, it paused in position. It paused in thought and reached no conclusion. Did it waver from its station or did the slow rise and fall of my breathing create the illusion of movement? In a house alone one must be very still. There was no sound. The cats were breathing. I regulated my own breathing carefully, slowly becoming aware of my pulse. I looked at it as if it was not happening to me, like I was looking out my window and into the apartment across the street. *Who's there? Nay, answer me: stand, and unfold yourself.* Not much unfolded.

I looked at it straight on. It was nothing, a misinterpretation of moonlight obscured on an overcast night, a double agent of my own invention, an apparition of dust and light playing on the wall and moving through me, allegiances both natural and unnatural. It was just my brain defragmenting: collecting and sorting the debris accumulated throughout the ordinary course of the day. It was just my brain defragmenting and encountering a glitch in the system. The imagination is colored, predisposed to shades of gray, a symptom of a vulnerable emotional state. If there was indeed a spirit in the room and it was what I was witnessing, I didn't anticipate convincing a jury on cross-examination.

I said nothing to anyone. At work, I began researching my apartment building via various online newspaper databases looking for a report of horrific events having transpired at my address. In *The New York Times*, I found the following article from March 12th, 1898: "Murder Mystery Solved Hilda Petersen Mother and Slayer of the Child That Was Found Dead at Rockville Centre. MAKES A FULL CONFESSION. A Swedish Servant Employed in This City Carried the Little Girl Away and Poured Carbolic Acid Down Her Throat." My address was mentioned in the article, but the crime didn't happen there. The father of the illegitimate child, a watchmaker, lived in my apartment with his five children and wife a century before me.

One night unpacking and organizing some boxes, I found a letter from my father, along with my reply.

July 1994
Dear Brett,

I can see that we are going to have some difficulty communicating over yesterday's drinking episode. I'm going to give the adult slant and you're going to try to give me the teenage spin. They are simply not compatible. Every kid in the world likes to think they are special, unique individuals, (and they are to some degree), but the situations they incur continue to be the same generation after generation. The talks I have with you are the same that my father had with me, and will be the same between you and your kids. I didn't want to hear it when I was your age, and I'm sure you don't want to hear it now. The bottom line is, I do have your welfare at heart. I love you and I want you to grow up to be as happy and successful as possible. You are bright, witty, and talented, but you are fifteen and nothing can change that but years. Without those years under your belt your judgment is skewed. You are still functioning on a teenage ego-trip, which only allows you to see how to get the things you want. And like most teenagers you'll manipulate and lie to get them. Also you will convince yourself that some of the most outrageous things are okay. Things like throwing parties in your father's house and driving around drunk. Hey, I'm not really as stupid as you think. I know these things. Fortunately to this point, as far as I know, most of your drives and desires have been handled within the law or at least with a bit of luck and without too much risk, I hope. But then I am not privy to much of your life. Parents are forced to do a lot of guesswork. Anyway I have given you a lot of trust. I have allowed you much leeway in your comings and goings. As a teenager, no doubt you believe everybody lets their fifteen-year-old go to DC on a whim, and head up to NYC on any given day. You know that just isn't the case. I have probably allowed too much to go by. And at times for selfish reasons like wanting to go away overnight. So I trusted you. I guess that really is not your fault, but mine. I should have known better. I chose not to see. I guess it's time that the door swings back. I do not condone kids drinking or using drugs. That the use is rampant is no excuse. It is bad policy for kids to do these things for both of the obvious reasons. They can be harmful both physically and psychologically and it's against the law. Believe me it is only a dumb kid argument to say the substances are not harmful. You know they are. You've seen the abuse. To say that you will not get caught is equally ridiculous. There is no crystal ball. And nobody is that smart, they just don't run out of luck. I see only bad things coming from drinking, smoking, and lying. None of those three will help you get by better in life. As I said, my hope for you is a healthy, happy, and successful life and I see that you are doing things that put those goals in jeopardy. As your father I have to do something to get you back on track. Hopefully you will understand that my judgment is not screwed up. Possibly you can see that I truly have your welfare in mind. In the past I have left many of the decisions up to you. I think I mistook your intelligence for maturity. I've done that before. I want to correct the error. Getting good grades is wonderful, but it doesn't buy you unlimited chances to screw up. To that end I am going to do my best to convince you that teenage drinking, smoking dope, and being untrustworthy are not in your best interest. I know what peer pressure is like. The brightest buckle under and actually believe that being staggering drunk, cursing out their father, and retching are cool. I hear the stories all the time. Still I want better for you. I don't want to get calls from the police department or, worse, the hospital. I've watched your brothers go through this, and maybe I've finally learned something. I've got to be, and I hate to say it, less trusting. Let's face it;

you've all lied to me. I guess I should expect it. For last night's performance I want you to give some serious thought to where you are going, and what is happening in your life. I believe the best way is to keep you in for a while. My decision is that you should stay in for five days. I won't take away your phone privileges this time, but next time you'll lose the phone and ten days of time. When your restriction is over, some new ground rules need to go into effect. I don't think it will be wise for you to spend the night at anybody's house. Because at this point I'll be thinking you are drinking. I'm not going to clip your curfew, but I will want you home every night at midnight. Over time, if you can build up my trust, this can be relaxed. If you can't get a ride, as usual, you can call me. I'm sure this will seem harsh to you, every punishment does, but I doubt it is much different than the rules that most fifteen-year-olds live by. Brett, trust and love are the foundation for relationships. I will be glad when we don't have to be adversaries. Until then I'll do what I have to do. I love you, and I hope you can regain my trust.

Love,
Dad

The night before I had arrived home with Elizabeth, a classmate I'd been dating for a week. We walked up the flight of steps into the condominium and my father was sitting in the living room. I attempted a high-five—a nonchalant gesture to demonstrate that all was well, I was not drunk, and nothing was out of the ordinary with my bringing an unfamiliar girl home near midnight. I missed the high-five and went to my bedroom to make out with Elizabeth, to kill time until her curfew.

Dad,

Please excuse my handwriting (my hand is broken from last night?). I waited around, then left because I didn't know if I was grounded or not. I understand your position in condemning my actions. In no way were they acceptable. But as a teenager I do do some things like that. Simon and Noah were into bigger and badder things than me and hey they're alright. I understand if those actions are repeated I will suffer and you would have to take some action as a parent. Even if you lose an argument with your opponent doesn't mean you still can't call them names.

I still love you,
Brett

My wrist was indeed broken—and not from a clumsy high-five with my father, but from punching my friend in his chest at a party the night before. It was a dare. We were in the basement of someone's house. It made a sort of sense at the time. We were drinking forties. I was posturing, and it escalated to its logical teenage conclusion: "I bet if you punch me as hard as your little ass could, I wouldn't even feel it." He was three times my size, the biggest in the room, one of my friends who was faithfully two steps behind me when I was drunk at a party, out of control, and spitting on a stranger. I didn't go to the doctor for a week—and then, once at the doctor, they needed to re-break the bone. My father photographed this event in the doctor's office—not from a parental impulse to document the pain I had caused myself by drinking, to have a record of my misdeeds, but because he had a disposable camera in his sport coat and it seemed like a funny thing to do.

I've recited the narrative of my addiction, the desperate and strange situations, so many times, it feels as if I'm reciting the first presidents using a mimetic device: What a Jolly Man Makes a Jolly Vixen. I can repeat the itinerary of my addiction; provide a cursory glimpse of childhood in a tone absent of any emotion or shock, having recited it numerous times in the rooms of professionals, on the first visit to a therapist or at Alcoholics Anonymous. "I did this. I did that." I begin in medias res like an epic poem:

There were times I was intoxicated and walked miles home with a black mind, and hours later could not recall walking home. I poured swigs of each liquor my father had in his cabinet—sambuca, vodka, kahlua—into a plastic sports bottle. I threw the bottle in my backpack and left for the weekend. Other times my jaw locked to the left or the right, filled with the anxiety of methamphetamines, leaving a pain that would remain for weeks after the night a white pill was swallowed in a room filled with strobe lights, filled with bodies, filled with music, filled with darkness. And mostly this is a matter of fact. It never lasted long enough. I would eat painkillers at lunch because drinking was too difficult, because the smell of weed would linger in the fabric of my clothing, and teachers could not easily identify the high of prescription pills. I smoked blunts driving around in a friend's car before school. Someone reported me and the nurse's office called for me in Algebra class. My heart rate was insane. I told the nurse I had three cups of coffee and she let me go back to class. I dropped acid at lunch, so when the last period bell rang and I walked out into a spring afternoon, I could sit for hours in a field of neon-tinted grass at Tyler Creek Park looking for a four-leaf clover. I drank forties and thought I could rap. We all did. I drank mushroom tea and played Sonic the Hedgehog, racing across the screen grabbing coins. I didn't smoke crack, though once I held an empty pipe to my lips as a joke. I was fishing for a reaction from my friends, who were with me in a living room where we were buying coke at three in the morning. If I hadn't noted their horror and feared their mentioning my actions the next week at school, it is possible I would have paid to refill the pipe. But we can play this game with anything. We drove home on River Road with the headlights turned off, curved along the Delaware River, miles from where George Washington crossed on Christmas Eve to surprise the British, miles from the spot where my family had watched the reenactment the previous Christmas morning.

There are no adequate similes or metaphors for addiction. There is no setting the broken bones back in place. And if there was, they wouldn't heal properly. The bones, forever injured, would develop a click in anticipation of dramatic changes in weather. With addiction, you simply know it when you feel it, when you admit it to yourself, and then, day by day, admit it to others in your life. Everything else is just an approximation, a literary device to advance an understanding, a voice of a loved one complaining. Or rather there is the addiction everyone else observes, and then there is the addiction the individual must come to terms with. It is an afternoon television special: *I don't have a problem. I can control it. I can stop if I want.*

When I was drunk there was a twenty-five percent chance I would cry and tell my friends they didn't understand the heights of my suffering. There was a twenty-five percent chance I would pick a fight, smash a window, or piss in the closet on a pile of dirty laundry. Or there was a fifty percent chance I would be fine and dance in the corner or play spades. There was no logic. I always had two bottles in my hand and a plan to raid the medicine cabinet of whatever house we were in. I didn't drink to cut the edge, to loosen up, to be right in the world—I drank to oblivion, to not remember anything or anyone.

It would be easy to say that my alcoholism was a weakness. That is the conventional narrative. But there are moments in which I want to admit that it was a power. A hero's singular ability to temporarily make the world invisible, to forget. I didn't want to remember. Perhaps here is where I should confess I wasn't loved enough, where I report that my genetic material was predisposed toward alcoholism, and worry over what I might have done to cause the difficulties and unhappiness in my parents' lives that weighed on me like a symbol, for the person I was doomed to become. There is my confession. I knew alcohol provided me with the power to avoid answering those questions, to eliminate them for an entire evening. There were no answers, and I wanted to be rescued from and defended against a world absent of them.

In 1996, at 7 AM in the basement of the University of Pittsburgh's Cathedral of Learning, I attended my first AA meeting. I had moved from the suburbs of Philadelphia to live with my brother Simon for the summer before starting my freshman year of college. He had started attending meetings three months earlier. He dropped me off on his way to work. I was barely awake. The other fifteen alcoholics were dressed for office jobs. At eighteen, in Pittsburgh, my recovery was a novelty. My bottom hadn't reached the horrific depths of the man who said he started snorting heroin because if he drank at work his boss would smell the alcohol on his breath. He had a wife, children, and a job—real responsibilities to fuck up. I'd barely had a job and didn't even have my driver's license. And yet I identified with such plots, the desperate way the mind warps to find and justify any method to obliterate feeling. Each addict's story provided a touchstone to my own life experience and there was something frighteningly sobering in the disastrous levels their addictions had reached. And I was relieved to know I wasn't alone, that there were others sitting beside me who were worse off.

Something can be called an addiction when it interferes with your life. That is what they say. My responsibilities as a teenager were limited. My father made sure I woke up on time for school, ignored each batch of fake throw-up I concocted from chewed-up cereal and a can of chicken soup, and stood at my bedroom door while I dressed. A third of the time that fake vomit worked— there were years I was absent from forty-something days of school. But in my household for the most part I did what was expected of me, and was lucky to avoid getting arrested, getting caught. When an actual *21 Jump Street*-style undercover police officer arrested three of my close friends in high school, I was waiting at the bus stop to buy mescaline dots from one of them. When his locker was searched and turned up a list of names with corresponding amounts of money next to them I was called down to the principal's office. The principal was a friend of my father's. If I had been caught, things could have been different.

The decision to admit the first of the twelve steps was easy. It had become transparent that I was powerless over alcohol at that particular moment in my life. The first several months went smoothly—I was physically removed from the triggers of old friends and places, of access to alcohol. I showed up at meetings once a day. I drank the Maxwell House coffee and ate the stale cookies and listened. I stood up and got a one month sober chip and people clapped.

I made no friends in AA or at college. My age made me an anomaly at meetings; I was too young to know the suffering of the world and "real" addiction and was treated more or less as such. As a freshman who didn't drink, I didn't leave my dorm room that often. On Saturday nights as the hallway filled with drunken cackles and the annoying voices of my peers, I sat alone in my room, shadows shifting down the hall visible through the crack at the bottom of the door. I made myself feel sorry for my peers in order to feel more mature, to feel superior to the people and activities I was no longer part of. I told myself they were exploring something for the first time that I'd discovered years ago. I was wiser. I was who I was because I refused what they were. And I had the battle wounds, and the morning meeting I attended while they were sleeping it off.

I listened to AM talk radio and fell asleep. Even in sleep I couldn't avoid the facts. For the first months of my sobriety, my brain formed dreams filled with drinking that were so vivid and haunting, featuring versions of real scenarios, that for weeks I was unsure if I'd relapsed. Even now, if asked how long I've been sober, I pause and question the fact. In the dreams I found myself wanting to avoid anyone I'd ever known—I would wake from a night of drinking and find myself at a department store with my father and an acquaintance from high school, the person whose bedroom wall I had punched or whose sister I had called a slut, or just the stranger whose name I couldn't remember even though they sat behind me in chemistry. In the dreams I felt compelled to say *I'm sorry. I'm different from last night. I'm sober now. I'm sorry.* And worse than the dreams was the waking guilt, the inability to swallow that guilt in drunkenness. For that first semester I dreaded going home for Christmas break, knowing the identity I had identified with was nowhere to be found.

I found another letter from my father while unpacking—this one from two or three years later, when I was in my second year of college, written in response to a phone conversation in which, possibly for the first time, I attempted to discuss my recovery and my ongoing depression. It's a strange thing about recovery—one is galvanized to finally address the years of behavior that, out of necessity, one was silent about. It is a little like holding a grudge over a friend's small slight or inattention and then months later exploding over a minor incident with disproportionate anger. Which is just to say, perhaps it was just my first step toward an adulthood being off on my own, my newfound sobriety, my first experience with therapy, or maybe my father had just telephoned on an evening I felt like talking. Whatever the case may be, I told him I wasn't doing well. And, perhaps as was characteristic of my family, my father responded with a letter.

Dear Brettski,

I sat back the other night and thought about what you told me about your depression etc. It is something you have kind of masked from me. Remember I've really only seen you a couple of times in the last nine months and our visits have been pretty brief, our conversations relatively superficial.

If it makes you feel any better (from the old misery loves company line of thinking), I went through many of the same feelings when I was in school. I certainly don't say that to minimize how you feel or what you are going through, but I do believe some of it is the maturing of an intelligent, sensitive young man.

It has always been difficult for me to make "close" friends. I don't suffer fools gladly. That meant for long stretches in my life I was alone, if not lonely. Particularly in college. I did have a few friends in the dorms, but as I've related in my stories to you, most were pretty weird guys. They were fringe characters, but interesting in their own way. I guess I was attracted to them, because they were not what I considered stupid folks, just eccentric. The "stupid" guys in my dorm are all now CEO's of large corporations. But I couldn't connect with them. Go figure.

There were times I pulled back and kind of shut myself up. I did a lot of reading, a lot of basketball by myself, and a lot of walking around Williamsburg. It was pretty depressing. When I got out of the dorm and I was living alone, I did some serious drinking. I was good and depressed a number of times and definitely contemplated offing myself. But then from time to time, I'd get my shit together and search out folks. That's how I got involved with theater. There were a bunch of goofy people there too, but at least many were interesting. If nothing else they were somebody to drink with, and of course there were always some pathetic characters that made my life look so much more worth living. But mainly I think my bad times were all due to my being too introspective. I'm afraid it's the bane of us pseudo-intellectuals. When I was selfishly thinking only about me, and my puny place in the world, when I only dealt with how things made me feel . . . it was pretty depressing.

As luck would have it, I fell into that job at Williamsburg's Eastern State Hospital. My approach to life started to change right away when I got involved in teaching. My emphasis shifted somewhat, but certainly not entirely, to the rest of the world, and specifically the kids I worked with. It didn't stop me from being cocky. It didn't mean I never thought about myself, but it did shift my focus away from me . . . me . . . me.

Obviously you and I are not the same. We only share millions of genes and some childhood experiences. Certainly many of our experiences are different, but some are more similar than you know. Similar enough for me to offer at least these suggestions. Try to look outward. Take what you have and share it with others. Don't force it; share it. Try to engage with other people in a caring considerate way. Try to do things for them. Basically I know you are already this way with your acquaintances. Make sure you do it with family and most certainly with girlfriends. Again I'm not 100 percent conscious of trying to do it. I don't want to sound preachy, but it's worked well so far.

I know turning your emotional outlook around is not easy. I don't mean to suggest that one little minor change and everything will be well, but I did feel that I wanted to share a little about my life in case it helps.

I know the Lauer boys (and their Mom) all love and care about each other. Hopefully we can all help each other out.

Love,
Dad

My problem with AA surfaced early. I had already done my time sitting in a circle listening to lectures that required I surrender to Krishna, godhead, to Him, to the program, to a higher being. My experience with groups suggested group logic prevails no matter how many times it is stated otherwise, as it is on the AA website, that "AA is not allied with any sect, denomination, politics, organization, or institution."

Through my sponsor I came to understand that there were options, intellectual wiggle room, other than the "He" and "Him" who appears in the language of the later steps—alternative ideas or substitutions that lead the addict to understand that he or she is not the center of the universe, to relinquish that control or narcissism, to place oneself humbly before something else. At one meeting, I shared my uncertainty in my beliefs regarding a conventional "higher power." I explained how I attempted to feel a comfort in the process of breathing ("breath" being from the Latin for "spirit"), and the knowledge that the cycle of the body continues unbeknownst to me. I am sleeping, and there it is keeping time. The man who spoke after me simply said: "God and Jesus are the higher power, youngster." Someone across the room said "Amen."

I wanted recovery, but I wanted to feel right in the world without the aid of a charismatic group or dogma. I had a chip in my hand marking a transition from the old life to the new, but I did not carry it in my pocket and rub it any time I had an urge to drink.

The truth is, I'd already exhausted my righteousness with straight-edge and Krishna Consciousness. I'd like to believe we are allotted a certain amount of such arrogance, hopefully spent entirely in our youth or expressed in the heat of the moment when a push-button topic divides a Thanksgiving Day table. The next day we wish we had reacted more humbly and generously to our aunt's neighbor regarding her view on capital punishment.

We can't go at it alone, and yet I needed to go at it alone, absent another belief system. "Humble yourself or be humiliated. Excuses are words put together to extinguish your guilt. Today will be here again tomorrow. It works if you work at it." The words of these new mantras were part of a system of indoctrination that I couldn't fully accept. I understood that if it wasn't for those rooms I wouldn't have been able to get sober, but I knew I needed to develop my own framework in which to understand myself in the world.

I've been sober for over a decade. I haven't been to a meeting in eight years. I've read that the human body replenishes all its cells on a seven-year cycle. Cells and atoms wear down and disappear or are replaced; skin flakes into the dust that surrounds us, resting on the windowsill. If this is the case, I'm no longer the same person after thirteen years of sobriety. I am almost doubly different. The transgressions and follies of youth are important to any life story: a cherry tree is chopped, St. Augustine steals a pear from an orchard, a boy runs off with a cult. These things happen in childhood, and you grow up and forget them, or you grow up and they haunt you, or, more than likely, you grow up and spend each morning dismissing the facts and waiting for your ghosts to appear.

I sat at my white desk. There was nothing to do but sit and wait. I put my legs up. I read *Baudelaire* by Jean-Paul Sartre. Above me on the wall was a framed print of Vishnu. I began the book in hopes of a close reading of Baudelaire's work and instead, twenty pages in, Sartre was still developing his psychoanalytic portrait of the poet:

> But the child who has become aware of himself as a separate being with a sense of despair, rage, and jealousy will base his whole life on the fruitless contemplation of a singularity which is formal. "You threw me out," he will say to his parents. "You threw me out of the perfect whole of which I was part and condemned me to a separate existence. Well, now I'm going to turn this existence against you. If you ever wanted to get me back again, it would be impossible because I have become conscious of myself as separate from and against everyone else." And he will say to his school-fellows and the street urchins who persecute him: "I'm someone else, someone different from all of you who are responsible for my sufferings. You can persecute my body, but you can't touch my 'otherness.'"

I bookmarked the page. I could say that Krishna Consciousness provided a framework, a coping strategy for the chaos of my childhood, for the age of Kali Yuga, the age of sin and vice lasting almost half a million years. Some of it stuck more so than AA, most likely because it got there first, because it was more complicated and mystical. The tradition of Krishna and its attractiveness to Westerners is no different than fascination with other Eastern religions—the appeal and fetishization of the esoteric, the exotic, and an "otherness." It sets itself apart—shaved heads, saffron robes, beatific faces dancing, playing cymbals, and chanting in an ancient language down Broadway at rush hour. It has all the signs of new-age crazy taking a wrong turn. However, I never quite experienced it that way. Of course there were rumors of cult-like brainwashing, or Krishnas involved in gun-running in the 70s, but the most I experienced was a feeling that the possibility of that zealous dogma was just around the corner, the dogma of any religion, of Evangelical Christians, of Hasidic Jews, that asks one to give up one's so-called "self" for a larger single-minded cause. But I didn't. I passed through. I was young and it was simple: there was a blue god, there was music, the devotees were happy and fulfilled, and not in a glazed-over way, and there was delicious food, but ultimately, I felt no different in or about the world.

I put down the book and looked at the image above my desk where Vishnu hovered above a lake, holding a lotus flower, a light haloing him. A crocodile retreated from an elephant it had attacked. The elephant's leg was bleeding. In his trunk he also holds a lotus. The elephant was Gajendra, the king of elephants. He was rescued from the crocodile because he was a devotee. In this moment of attack he prayed not to be saved from the crocodile, but from this life of ignorance. He struggled, some say for a hundred years, and only after his family left him at the edge of the pond, thinking death was imminent, did he pray. Many years later on September 11, or driving in a blizzard, or on an airplane in the moment before lift-off, or before falling asleep, without thinking I chanted the Maha Mantra, like a lullaby. *Hare Krishna Hare Krishna Krishna Krishna Hare Hare Hare Rama Hare Rama Rama Rama Hare Hare.* I was hoping the transcendental vibrations would still the psychological ones.

Soon I came to anticipate the ghost's presence in my apartment: watchmaker father, the murdered child, her mother Hilda, or otherwise. I smoked cigarettes at my computer and waited for nightfall, gathered myself for bed, forgot to eat. I grabbed another book—what else was there to do—and read a poem in Rimbaud's *A Season in Hell:*

> On the roads on winter nights, homeless, half-naked, hungry, I heard a voice that gripped my frozen heart: "Weak or strong: there you stand, and that is strength. You don't know why or where you're going; enter anyplace, answer everyone. No one's going to kill you, any more than if you were a corpse." The morning, I looked so lost, so dead in my eyes, most likely everyone I met never saw me at all.

For three consecutive nights the ghost clung to the exact same spot. I had done my research. I had contemplated purchasing devices that measured changes in the air, humidity, positive and negative ions, barometric pressure; that could pinpoint warm, cold, or bright spots, or disturbances in the electronic field. If one wanted surefire proof, night vision goggles were an available option, as were chimes to measure the movement of a spirit, if placed at an appropriate distance from natural drafts. Mostly, during the day, I read articles about the murder in *The New York Times* and *The Evening Telegram* online archives.

> My name is Hilda Peterson and I live at No. 58 East Fifty-Third Street, I have been employed there for three weeks and have been in the country for four years. I became acquainted with Charles Johnson the first year I was here. I met him in Brooklyn. Afterward we became intimate, and a girl baby was born. She was named Annie. He was the child's father. Subsequent to the birth of the child I did housework. I put the

baby to board with a family in DeKalb Avenue, Brooklyn. I had Johnson arrested and he was ordered to pay $2 a week to the Charities Commissioners to support the child.

Her daughter had been found:

in a chicken run . . . dressed only in a knitted undershirt and black stockings, fastened with elastics. The child was well developed, and well nourished, beautifully formed, and handsome, having large gray eyes and long, waving blonde hair. The chicken run is a square box made of slats, five feet long by two and a half square, and is used to allow young chickens air and exercise. . . . It was evident that the child had been killed by a heavy dose of carbolic acid. . . .

Hilda was depicted as calm, sane, and with "no indication of distress or remorse," as she confessed:

It was still snowing a little. There were some houses near the station, so I took Annie up a couple of blocks into some place and gave her the carbolic acid. I don't remember whether she swallowed it or not but she lived only a few minutes. When she was dead I pulled her clothes and threw them along the ground. I took her shoes and brought them home and put them in my trunk.

I was living and sleeping in Charles Johnson's apartment, the absent father of the murdered daughter, or at least the plot where his house once stood at the turn of the century. My ghost detective logic led me to believe Hilda was in the house with me, haunting Charles, the descendants of Charles, the domestic life in the New World that was denied her. Or rather that was the possibility I allowed, since the size and shape of my ghost discounted Annie. That is, if one believes how one dies is how one haunts. It might work this way: Those who died in dungeons drag their chains, those in straitjackets forgotten in a mental institution continue their screaming, or the man who met his death on the guillotine carries his head cradled gently against his waist. I could find no record of Hilda's death. The last article in my searches reported on her arraignment; and on the same newspaper page, in the column directly adjacent her story, a new story was beginning, that of a different family and another child found lifeless in a trunk.

They say that when one is weak illness attacks. I will not, at this present moment, go on record as believing in such things as apparitions traveling through keyholes, doorknobs turning and turning, disembodied voices whispering—all proof of vagrants held captive to wander the prison-house of the material world as reminders of the misdeeds they were subjected to. I remember a Krishna devotee speaking of waking up and being clamped by demons. He was barely able to mouth the mantra: *Hare Krishna Hare Krishna Krishna Krishna Hare Hare Hare Rama Hare Rama Rama Rama Hare Hare*, and then the demon fled. I kept the mantra on my lips in case the ghost approached.

My mind transformed a shadow into a visitation. There was a strange comfort in the shadow's existence. It did not harm me, it knew that I would die, that we all will die, and there was comfort in this inevitability. It conveyed the obvious—there are worse lives, circumstances. There is, after all, no rush—despite the anxiousness to deplane a recently landed aircraft, we exit in the order we are placed. Row by row, our turn arrives. The edge of the cliff we will fall off is always right there in the last place we look, like misplaced keys. What does not harm you only makes you calmer. I thought: *The seasons continue to change and you will be with me, my friend.*

She was there and then she was gone. I want to believe I was there for her and she was there for me, that even the undead were searching for some other to confirm their existence. It is what we do when we're alone in the world.

3

My friends either told me it was too soon to start dating or that the grass was growing tall beneath my feet. It had only been six months since my separation. The last time I was single, the world anxiously watched the news for reports of missile systems misfiring as the year ticked into the new millennium. Postage was 33 cents. *NSYNC was touring and it wasn't a reunion. The world had changed, and even if it hadn't, I wouldn't have been any more adept at courtship. I dated my first real girlfriend on and off from middle school until I was a sophomore in college. The beginning of our courtship involved moments standing awkwardly beside each other at a friend's bar mitzvah and talking on the phone until two in the morning about The Smiths, our parents, movies. I sent her hundreds of love letters, which she later burned. I'm sure it was deserved. And when that ended, it was only a few brief months before I was in a relationship with Nina.

I never would have approached Nina, and in fact it was Nina who approached me at a friend's party and asked me to dance. I was at the party to be set up with a different friend-of-a-friend, Stephanie, and at the end of the evening when we shared a cab home I couldn't bring myself to ask Stephanie for her number. What can I say? I'm shy. I'm insecure. I couldn't even maintain eye contact with a woman walking by me on the street. I feared rejection and the possibility that my male gaze (I'd taken one survey class on feminism in college) was offensive and an objectifying intrusion. I wouldn't want to make anyone uncomfortable with my advances, silent eyeballs or otherwise. I didn't let my eyes linger on a sheer shirt and black bra. I watched the eyes of other men; watched them turn around halfway up the block to look at an ass in short shorts, watched them trail everywhere after everyone. I was satisfied smelling perfume as a woman passed. And so Stephanie drove into the night without me and I remember the scent of the woods and fig leaves.

But it was spring, that heady time in the city when we tell ourselves we should be outside walking on a promenade, or sitting under a blooming tree, identifying our own lives with the shifts in meteorological patterns. My divorce was being finalized and I found myself at Jess and Todd's apartment, and the computer was on Jess's lap and she was signing me up for a dating site. It started simply enough. I didn't resist, besides a requisite roll of my eyes and shoulder shrug, as we flipped through *The Collected Poems of Wallace Stevens* and John Ashbery's *Hotel Lautréamont*, playing a parlor game with my dating profile, finding chance phrases and lines that both amused us and provided a possible answer to the question being asked. A distant third consideration was whether the phrase, plucked at random, sufficiently represented my sensibility, or the sensibility we were crafting for me. There was no harm in signing up—the act itself didn't necessitate my active participation in the dating life. In the end my profile read in part:

- The best or worst lie I've ever told: The apples fall without astronomy.
- The role religion plays in my life: He felt curious about the winter hills.
- Why you should get to know me: Prefers the brightness of bells, imperceptible errors, and a speech of the self that must sustain itself on speech.
- If I was given a million dollars: A little island full of geese and stars.
- More about what I am looking for: Canaries in the morning, orchestras. My heart pinned in a trance to the notice board.

We included the bare minimum of facts:

- The last thing that made me laugh out loud: Doing this.
- If I could be anywhere right now: New York City.

- Five items I can't live without: Books, my cats, coffee, my friends, the artificial world.
- My personal style: Sexy casual.
- Body art: None.
- Favorite item of clothing: Glasses.
- In my bedroom one will find: A deer decal, a sleeping cat, books.
- The last great book I read: Wallace Stevens's *Collected Poems*.

Following the fill-in-the-blanks there was a series of true or false questions. "People ask you for dating/sex advice." "I love to host dinner parties/board game nights/orgies, etc (where 'etc' is your activity of choice)." "My heart controls my brain (among other organs)." "When I'm in a relationship, I believe there's always room for improvement." "I like to grasp the details first, then big picture later." "I'm a head-in-the-clouds kind of person." False. False. False. True. True. False. And just like that, my so-called "romantic profile" was revealed to be the "Gentle Artist":

> You are nature's balm: the soothing presence who calms us when we are stressed, who reminds us of the delightful spontaneity of childhood, and who shows us how to appreciate nature and all living things. But as easily as you bring happiness to others, you can bring sadness to yourself when you fail to see your strengths, focusing only on your limitations.
>
> Love for you is an all-or-nothing experience. Because you tend to shut out the rest of the world so you can experience love more fully, you can be vulnerable to the whims of your beloved. Devotion and flexibility are two of the most important qualities you, as a Gentle Artist, bring to a relationship. You can meet the Gentle Artist everywhere art, fashion, nature, children, and animals are present or discussed.

There wasn't much else to do or learn about myself—my curriculum vitae completed, now I needed to apply for the job. We hovered around the computer on Jess's lap and disagreed about who was or wasn't attractive. We made pronouncements like: "Who wants to be with a hedge fund broker?" or "I hate yoga," or "She looks like she could be your sister." The night ended and I rode the N train home and signed back in, this time with the necessary privacy to determine my own dating qualifications.

It wasn't an easy task—the dating site was a rabbit hole, each profile picture labeled "Click Me." Click Me: "Sugar on Spikes." Click Me: "New in Town." It was a frenzy of clicking, self-doubt, arrogance, lust. *I wouldn't have sex with her. Or would I? She is too good for me. She wouldn't have sex with me. Her favorite movie is* Father of the Bride? I refreshed the dating site. I stared out my window at the skyline waiting. I sat pressing F5, the site reloading a fresh grid of faces. Click Me: "What's wrong with a little self-destruction?"

I might be of the last generation born without full immersion in and preoccupation with technology. I played the early computer game Oregon Trail, followed green dots to safety. I wrote all my college papers on a Brother word processor with a two-inch preview screen that fit three lines of text. The total disclosure of my personal life wasn't my natural state. It felt foreign, strange, and awkward. I was more adept at watching the stream of comments and posts than with sticking my foot in to test the waters. I'm not saying I walked uphill both ways in the snow to the church dance to hold my steady's hand through a white glove, only that I did believe we were meant to meet our friends and lovers the old-fashioned way. Via college, the workplace, at a bookbinding class, a third-party introduction, or at a café on Sunday, sitting patiently reading a book all afternoon anticipating someone would notice.

Instead, I was inside devising searches by height, age, and location to generate a photo of someone new. It was spring outside on the avenues, a parade was happening somewhere in the city and I thought: *Let the couples who find themselves outdoors observe that it is spring. Let them be intoxicated with noting that it is spring, pointing out flowers about to bud, and wandering with their golden retrievers to cafés serving microbrews.* When logged in, my photo appeared on the homepage for others who were logged in. *I'm watching you watch me flickering on the screen in what looks like an orchard or pumpkin patch. A left arm is around your waist. The body of a stranger is cropped out. Your ex-boyfriend's phantom wristwatch is still glimmering in the corner.*

I posted another photo. I learned it was important to post several photos, current, and in good lighting, preferably wearing a shirt. I wanted women to think I was serious and beautiful. I posted a photo in which I was wearing, please forgive me, a fedora and looking past the photographer. There I was, positioned according to the rule of thirds, with the Empire State Building lit up over my shoulder out the window in the background. In the final photo, I was in Jess and Todd's kitchen wearing a Halloween mask of a horse's head.

The first email I received was a single sentence:

Please describe an "imperceptible error."

Mary

I wrote back:

Dear Mary,

That's a good question, but to answer adequately I might need to sketch diagrams and would definitely require a dry erase board. But I will give it a go; it is, after all, in my profile. I would say imperceptible errors are the errors which define a person, and in defining are imperceptible as parts. They are what make the person who she or he is and adds to their charm. I just looked up "error" in the Oxford English Dictionary. Its original meaning was "to wander," as in Alfred Lord Tennyson's "The damsel's headlong error thro' the wood." I like the idea of wanderings which cannot be "apprehended with the mind or senses" or be captured. How is that?

Brett

Dear Brett,

I'd like to see some Venn diagrams and maybe a Gantt chart. Are you saying "quirks"? To me, quirks don't equal errors. I was thinking imperceptible errors would be like, very tiny mistakes that add up over time and then climate change happens or your stove explodes. Bad examples, maybe. I can see how wander would come to mean error. It's interesting it would go from literal to figurative like that.

Do you like poop?

Sincerely,
Mary

I emailed a different girl, and she emailed me, then I emailed her, then she emailed me, and then I emailed her. Soon almost a week had passed without a reply. *She's busy. She's dating someone else. She noticed I'm divorced. Note to self: That horse head photo is a distinct sign of creepiness and not whimsy. Buyer beware. We would never work out. She lives in Hoboken.* But a virtual brush-off was still a brush-off. So I checked Craigslist Missed Connections, a virtual bulletin board of personal classifieds written by individuals who met or momentarily noticed someone else across a crowded train or in line at a movie, but due to whatever particular chain of events—train doors opening before the nerve to speak arrived, a phone number lost to the washing machine—they were unable to contact that person directly. One could write a post about the moment in hopes of reconnecting, if indeed the other party happened to find the post and was interested. I felt safe checking Missed Connections. My voyeurism was protected. There was no real expectation of being located and understood, no photos of prospective dates, no pressure to psych myself up to write a witty introductory email.

It was a fairy tale, a distraction that allowed one to believe a letter in a bottle was washing up on the distant mythical shores of Atlantis, where every single woman was beautiful: in tights and cowboy boots, red flats and a black miniskirt, a tattoo of a star on her wrist, a broken heart on her arm, skinny gray jeans and white sneakers on the train. But I was never anywhere—at 2 AM I was asleep, not dancing at Home Sweet Home. I didn't shop at Whole Foods on Tuesday with a green tote or ride a mountain bike across the bridge. I rode the subway to work. I had baby blue high-top sneakers, rectangular tortoise frame glasses. I didn't want to be overlooked. Someone must have seen me. "We sat across from each other. You were reading *The Year of Magical Thinking*. I was reading *Regarding the Pain of Others*. You got off; I wanted to say something." It would be one thing to be noticed—to inspire intrigue or wonder, eyes not passing over me but pausing to con-template a little further who I was, feeling the blush rise around my neck. It was a gigantic other thing to have that person follow up, an hour later, three days in the future, unable to shake thoughts of what a voice sounded like, so that in the middle of the night or a lull during work, the interaction is typed, a descriptive missive floating out into the Internet's cosmos. I told my friend Charlie that when a person does this in an attempt to find you, you are at the peak of your desirability. It should not be squandered.

I was vigilant. It was important to remember each person I exchanged chitchat with was a possible Missed Connection. A woman approached me at the coffee shop. "I think you dropped this." I was caught off-guard. I looked at her left hand for a wed-ding band. Todd told me that Missed Connections don't happen, you make them happen. "I like your scarf. I just finished reading that book." Pathologically pathetic, I held the door open for anyone. I tucked in my shirt. I wanted to be presentable. I had difficulty smiling at strangers. One day I walked past Parker Posey and made eye contact. We were on our cell phones. *Let it start to rain so we can duck under the same awning to wait for the storm to clear, let the rain fall as I walk on without an umbrella stepping on every electrical manhole waiting for the stray voltage to notice me and knock me dead.*

I got back to my apartment and checked Missed Connections out of loneliness and boredom, which are the same. There is a beauty in anonymous strangers reaching out into the ether to find someone they believe they have shared a moment with—a cab from the airport, a phone number smudged off a sweaty hand. I wanted to find faith in others looking for each other—and not just the "you bought me and my friends a drink at an anonymous bar" types, but romance, or an uncanny quality in how, in a city of millions of characters, there is bound to be a story starting some-where. But once I had read them for a week, for two weeks, for a month, the stories began to sound the same. If a dating profile was the curated language one was required to enter in order to participate, a list of likes and dislikes and witty phrases crafting an identity we hope another will share or find value in, then the Missed Connection was just another outlet for longing, and the longing had carved out its own genre. In the end, the algorithm for online dating is just a pretext. It's not perfect and it doesn't matter. I had pretended to subvert the process when creating my dating profile, but that was just a trick to get myself to feel comfortable with participating. So there I was. My phone wasn't ringing. *Nothing is happening. I must make something happen.*

I composed a fake Missed Connection from the headlines and marketing slogans of the dating site, using words that others had selected to present themselves to the world, to prove they were lovable.

SUBJECT: Rain or Shine / m4w / Brooklyn

It may or may not be unfortunate that people search for certain sex, anonymous travels, individuals for laughter, or text messaging all night. It takes time to write these emails with a personal account reduced to various forms of opportunities and objects I can't account for. Click here: just what you never knew you were going to get, a girl prowling about town, sugar on spikes, what's wrong with a little self-destruction, placing the ass in Cassidy since 1979. Set standards, and bingo, break 'em. It takes time to uncover each other, start off and finish the walk in the park, later dismiss the passage or the symphony heard on the barge circling sirens from the island. It may be artificial, it is artificial, but I won't shoot myself footless, brave waters in a kayak and some shy garment. Others are determined to attend fashion week or a free bluegrass concert on an abandoned pier. I swear I want this whole world, just not most of that. Let's just talk about this sunset, or the rosy fingers of dawn, better still dirty-talk if you say so, both of us, at once, starting now. It may end up being a touch to never scrub away. This may or may not be mutually beneficial, but here I am, two miles away, your three-night stand, rain or shine, on foot.

And, small World Wide Web that it was, Cassidy responded:

Dear Mr. Mystery Missed Connection,

I'm not sure if your post had anything to do with me, but my friend passed it along because my MySpace tagline is "putting the ass in Cassidy since 1979." Although fashion week and bluegrass concerts aren't ringing a bell, that's potentially my ass you're talking about. Have we met?

Cassidy

Dear Cassidy,

I don't know you. I wrote the Missed Connection based on profiles from a dating site. It was meant to be a project to see if I could take all the interesting language and tag-lines and craft it into a text that represented that strange experience. Perhaps I didn't think it all the way through. I didn't expect you'd stumble upon it, and hope it didn't freak you out too much. I'll remove the posting if it did.

Jake

Hey Jake,

It's no problem—I was mostly bewildered, since 90% of the entry was unfamiliar (. . . but since I was at McCarren Pool twice this week, I figured I would check it out). It's pure luck that I have a friend that peruses Missed Connections! Don't worry about taking it down. It's not really deprecatory, just odd. I do feel sheepish for being busted for being on a dating site, though.

Cassidy

Cassidy,

Oh, don't feel sheepish. You got "caught" by someone who is also on the site. That doesn't really count. Also, to come clean, and make this entire thing even more creepy, my name isn't Jake.

Yours,
Brett

It took me three weeks to realize my aimless and compulsive clicking throughout the dating site had consequences. Each click was recorded. Every person I clicked on could see that I had been viewing her profile, had clicked through her slideshow of four photos. There were few photos on the site I hadn't spent time contemplating. Let's face it; there wasn't much else to initially go on, and the fact that someone was looking at my profile was a form of interaction. An affirmation. Even if we were all trigger-happy, clicking away until dawn, still I was relieved to know others found the miniature image of my face worth the minimal effort of pressing their pointer finger down on the mouse. Maybe I shouldn't have been so reckless with my clicking, but "sending a wink" seemed immature, silly—having a middle school friend ask a girl if she thought I was cute, while I held down mute on the three-way call. *I should just take the chance and email the person.* I wanted to start each email: "Forgive my trespass of your personal space and please don't feel obligated to reply to this note in which I demonstrate that I have read 'your' and not 'you're' profile, and have spelled everything correctly, despite my ugly habit of homonym mistakes." It did, I admit, feel good to be "hot-listed," even by women with fuzzy matchbook-sized photos. Each click straightened my slumping shoulders. I set a goal of 1,000 views. I'd "hot-listed" fifty-seven people. That seemed like too many. It was just a list to return to, like bookmarked websites or an online shopping cart—I could decide tomorrow whether or not it was imperative I own gray desert boots, maybe I should wait to see if my sudden interest in Russian icons wanes. It was also a way to let the other person know I was interested, that I was there and available. I signed in and wrote a note to Daphne, with whom I had already traded a few emails.

August 17, 2007
Dear You,

I guess it was forward and inappropriate for me to ask you over
last night, to place you in a position where you felt there could be
any danger to your well-being, and I am sorry I did that. And your
co-worker of course was right, you shouldn't show up alone at a
strange boy's house in the middle of the night to watch Japanese
anime, a million terrible things could happen, and often do, and I
guess I felt somehow like it wasn't quite a first meeting, that with
the illusion of the connectedness of the Internet I somehow knew
you more than a complete stranger. But I guess that is true and
not true. You don't really know me yet, and I don't know you, and
it would be better to do that in a safe location. It 3:30 AM and I
am in a safe location and thinking about sleeping and meeting
you tomorrow or today actually as I write this and you read it.
There are helicopters hovering over the projects. The night is over,
for me at least. Maybe you are still awake. Maybe you will get
this before morning, though I hope not. Tomorrow we will walk
around in public at the zoo and talk and nothing will come of
it or else I won't be able to tell. And I have said enough already.
I'm feeling pretty ridiculous at this point. I think most people
are laughing at me. Especially you. That's fine. For now. I guess.
Though not for much longer. And yeah we can get to know each
other and look at all the caged birds, and animals, pretending they
are happy. I think I will not expect anything. I will expect to say
hello and talk and see what you have to say, and tell you things.
And then, goodbye. I know these things take time, and I won't
place that pressure on myself, or you, or is that what these emails
are meant to do? I'm feeling a little sad today. I'm not sure why. I
wish I wasn't divorced and that my refrigerator was full.

Brett

August 17, 2007
Dear Bretton,

I don't want you to feel sad. I honestly don't care that you are divorced or have nothing in your fridge. I'm single and have expired everything in mine. I mean I was dating someone for about 7 months not long ago and all those feelings and the closeness that I thought I had with him was obviously nothing. I'm by myself now and it makes me feel dumb. I mean that's nothing to what you have been through so it makes me dumb to even say anything. I like your heavy emails.

Daphne

August 18, 2007
Dear Daphne,

I know you think my attention and affection are not merited yet in the situation, on account of it being so soon, that you feel disconnected from it and that makes you sad, and that makes me question myself and my own actions. Am I just sweet and that is how I interact in the world, or am I more like how I think you are perceiving me: desperate for love? And maybe it is both. And that makes me sad, to know that about myself or even imagine that about myself. And if it is true, what do I do with it? Slow down little pony. I tend to gallop. And I will try to rein myself in a little, though it will be difficult. As last night proved. I guess in that regard I am a boy lying next to a pretty girl and my body takes over and seems to fit too nicely with yours. I don't want you to regret anything or think about it the next day with dread. I want you to be excited about me, about seeing me, sleeping next to me. And it made me sad on the subway to see you strange and sad talking about your ex-boyfriend.

All of that,
Bretton

August 20, 2007
Dear Bretton,

I don't think you are desperate for love. . . . I mean maybe we all are a bit, including me but not in the evil way you are thinking. I think you are like me, you fall easily. The amount of affection does make me feel a little empty . . . and it has nothing to do with you. It's just odd to me. . . . But since you have gone through what you have—that makes me question how you can be so affectionate with me. I think you are just an extra sweet and emotional guy. Nothing in the world wrong with that. I like hanging out, I just hate the empty stupid feelings I get when I, for lack of better term, "mess around" with someone. It's not you, it's me. I don't know why I get like that. The extra affection that I don't know the source of makes me confused. I don't know how to reciprocate that. And I don't blame your friends for telling you it's too early to date, but how can they give you advice for something they have not lived through? And you should not be sad and stuck in your house. It's not healthy. It's also not healthy to jump from relationship to relationship . . . I'm having fun and you are too so that's what matters. And I was a little bummed that you said we might not hang out because you wanted space, because I want to hang out. I wanted a picnic and I sort of want to see you today. That's nothing new. Wish you were online, bleh.

Daphne

I had the month of August off from work and so I was available
to spend a good deal of time with Daphne. My days were free. I
rode the subway with her to work in the morning, met her at the
end of the day and rode back to her apartment and straight to her
room. We lay in bed and ordered food and movies. There was a
canister of Easy Cheese permanently on her bureau, it could have
been half-empty or half-full; I never saw it in action. We went
to the zoo. We held hands. She had beautiful eyes. She bought
me my own boyfriend pillow when I began ending up with hers
in the morning. She was the first person to send me images that
made me blush—I squinted at my tiny LG flip phone screen to
take it all in. She began to call me her "pretend" boyfriend, an
acknowledgment, I think, that we were playing house. I think she
liked having me there as much as I liked being somewhere. I'd
only dated a few people after the divorce and she was recently
out of a relationship, and we were trying to make sense of what it
was like to be caring and cared for. The "pretend" helped us both
impersonate love, until, of course, it no longer did.

September 3, 2007
3:21 PM

DAPHNE: I don't like you emailing people on Nerve.

ME: I know you don't.

DAPHNE: Well, quit emailing. I like having a pretend boyfriend, it works for me. I can't share.

ME: Well then, it isn't pretend, is it?

DAPHNE: I prefer it pretend. You have too many issues for it to be real. If one of us finds someone more awesome, fine, but you shouldn't be emailing around each day because you can. That's lame.

ME: Where do you think finding someone else is going to happen?

DAPHNE: If you are emailing around that is just like telling the world "Here I am" and it makes it easier for you to poof! and disappear, but if you are dealing with real life you will be too busy hanging out with me to ever meet anyone.

ME: And real life is a pretend relationship?

DAPHNE: Yes. You're too shy to meet anyone in real life unless they are whoring it up and in that case they will be trashy.

ME: So I should be spending all my time with you. That sounds like you have me in your clutches.

DAPHNE: Pretty much. I like it that way. I'm very selfish.

ME: You want something which is totally understandable but something I'm not willing to give you.

DAPHNE: Ok.

ME: Right?

DAPHNE: Yes. I said Ok.

ME: I mean we could try to see each other more casually.

DAPHNE: No. I'm not capable of that. I have a bad problem jumping into things like no one's business. I'm very dysfunctional. I'm a serial hang-arounder, but I can actually stand you and you aren't an addict or an asshole. I promise you I don't like most people. I have a feeling though that you fall easily and it must feel nice for you right now because you are so starving for affection.

ME: Some of that might be true. I mean, I guess it is. Some of that.

DAPHNE: Well at least you got some nice affection that will hold you over a bit.

ME: I don't think about it that way.

DAPHNE: Well it's the way I said. You are being all true to yourself! You go boy! Dr. Phil would be very proud.

ME: Thanks Daphne.

DAPHNE: I really can't be your friend. I've let you know how I feel.

ME: I understand.

DAPHNE: If I was awesome I would be your friend, because that's what you do if you like someone, but I'm all or nothing unfortunately.

ME: Maybe you will be able to at some point, just not today or next week.

DAPHNE: No I won't. I'm very good at eliminating people, for lack of a better word. I don't want to be your friend. I don't want to see you dating around. I won't be happy for you. And I don't want to wait around while you find other stepping stones to maybe one day want to hang out with me more, that's gross. Whatever, look how fast and out of nowhere you did this to me; wanting affection and being cute isn't a good combo to avoid that kind of stuff. It's romantic and unabashed and vulnerable blah blah blah. Thanks. You are kind of dumb because I'm the coolest girl you will ever meet.

ME: Ok.

DAPHNE: You are going to have a hell of a time dating people. Because anyone ok with you fucking around is going to be dumb and have AIDS. Don't be offended, but I am deleting you off email, Facebook, etc. You should write a girl back and meet someone to stay distracted, it will help.

ME: I can't deal with rehashing how much of an asshole and wrong and fucked up and cruel I am.

DAPHNE: You aren't, really.

ME: So I'm just going to get AIDS?

DAPHNE: Well with the situations you want, yes you are. You are fishing around a crummy pool of people.

ME: I told you I don't know that I will be dating, and if and when I do I will set up parameters to keep things from getting serious.

DAPHNE: That's impossible. You tried to set up parameters with me. People don't work that way. Hello. Blah. I feel like I'm going to cry.

ME: What can I do?

DAPHNE: This makes me think you are a pretty crummy person and that I have been duped. I'm beginning to hate your fucking guts.

ME: You can think that if it makes it easier to think I'm a fuck-face. But that isn't true. And I'm sorry that there were some things that were crummy and didn't work out. But I wasn't dishonest or disingenuous with you at all.

DAPHNE: Ok. Fuck off. Thanks for fucking me. Glad I could get another guy off.

ME: Are you done?

DAPHNE: You really added more fucked up shit to my lovely record.

ME: Don't hold me accountable for your record.

DAPHNE: You are part of it now. The end result is always the same. Go fuck some girls to get it out of your system. I thought you weren't like that. Asshole. But guess what, you are! Hooray for me!

ME: That isn't true.

DAPHNE: If it makes you feel better to tell yourself that then go ahead.

ME: It is taking all my power to not tell you to go fuck yourself.

DAPHNE: I'm not making anything up, it's true. Did it take all your power to fuck me and know you didn't want anything more?

ME: You had every opportunity to end it.

DAPHNE: You just want to keep doors open with various people, yet sleep with me. That makes sense.

ME: You can go ahead and chalk me up as some boy who is out there fucking around. I don't think that is true, and didn't ever treat you that way.

DAPHNE: Facts are facts.

ME: You are the first person I have been with after my divorce. I'm sorry.

DAPHNE: So what. Lucky me, oh lucky me.

ME: Please stop. I'm at work. Can we talk about this later?

DAPHNE: THIS ALWAYS HAPPENS. You should have left me alone and known not to fuck a girl who has told you this is what happens to her. Don't do it again, asshole, to someone else when you know you can't do anything but jump around from person to person. It's not fair to others.

ME: Lesson learned.

DAPHNE: You are playing with people and that's so fucked up. You should take down your fucking profile.

ME: You are treating me like someone I'm not.

DAPHNE: Facts are facts.

ME: Don't blame me for them.

DAPHNE: Do you know how long it has been since I've slept with someone sober?

ME: That is fucked up, and not my fault.

DAPHNE: Or with someone who actually liked me? You walked into a train-wreck. Just leave girls alone.

ME: Fine. I will. I've clearly no grasp.

DAPHNE: The worst part is you just think it's cool by saying: "Hey I'm so nice. I don't do this to people." Just say: "Yes, Daphne, I knew I couldn't do anything more, but I was real nice to you and spent a lot of time with you and made you think there was actually something there and I fucked you because it had to be done. There had to be a first after my divorce. I knew it would end up with nothing, but I need to start somewhere."

ME: Fuck you.

DAPHNE: Stop fucking around with girls.

ME: Ok. Fine. Done. I have work to do.

I told myself it was an untenable position. *I should stay home, stare at the brownstones across the street, search the computer screen for new books and ties, make a cup of tea, watch a movie, go to bed, wake up and clean up the cat fur with a Swiffer.* In the heat they never stopped shedding, even the ceiling fan somehow managed to gather their fur on its blades. The cats begged to be brushed, and then the fur didn't stop coming off. It gave me something to do. A task to complete. Maybe, as friends suggested, I wasn't "ready" to be dating. Is anyone ever prepared for anything? Maybe the Buddhists, with a mind detached from desire and ignorance sitting quietly watching the material world pass.

I saw only two options: either I would live with loneliness or continue to attempt to make connections and fail, in any number of new ways. I couldn't allow myself to be interested in every new person I dated. It had only just started and already it was exhausting, a math equation across a chalkboard devised to prove its own difficulty. It would be a series of failures until it wasn't. I was broken and slowly fitting the pieces into some self that could walk through the door. And I walked through the door. And yes, I fell too easy; a sweet word shattered me into a thousand shards. And what was I supposed to do with this? How to settle into anything, without awkwardness, with the earth at a slight tilt and me leaning against the wall avoiding the eyes of others? And what does anyone really need but an email in the morning from a stranger that says "Tell me about yourself."

The more time I spent combing through profiles the less weird it felt, and I became a little braver in contacting people. I showed up for the dates, was there on time or five minutes early, smiled, carried on a conversation, asked questions, laughed as I paused to sip my coffee. I was forever sipping coffee at a café on a first date since I couldn't bring myself to meet at a bar—I was less worried about relapsing than giving off what I feared was a distinctly creepy vibe of not drinking while my date was, me standing too close and too sober as if at any minute I was going to spike her drink with Rohypnol. It might have been a sense of arrogance, a misguided male characteristic in a city populated with more women than men, or my insecurity masquerading as confidence, my timid standoffishness misread as self-importance, but I came to view myself as an average catch in the world of Internet romance. What I mean to say, to clarify, is that it was enough to not be a complete fucking monster—the people I met had come to expect another awful encounter in a series of awful encounters. I exhibited a strict personal policy of not yelling at my dates on our first meeting. I didn't ask if "they always dressed so slutty." I didn't get up for another drink and never return. I hadn't been unemployed for years. My hand didn't drift to their neck with a hateful grip when we were kissing. These were all real experiences relayed to me on dates. I learned this was something to talk about on first dates—all our past dates from the site were an experience we bonded over.

And though I understood there was a world of dating in which two people fooled around and it meant nothing, with me, it turned to something else quickly. They saw the absence of harm, they saw potential, and they thought I might be the one to settle down with for a period of time. I wasn't complaining. So what if I spent the entire weekend with them in bed, at the farmers' market, ordering Thai food? I wanted to be that person, thought I was that person, needed to believe I was the boyfriend type. I couldn't stand to see myself as anything else.

September 4, 2007
9:30 AM

ME: On my way to work from girl's apartment.

CHARLIE: Yeah man, how did you swing that?

ME: No idea, magic or something. But what's the worst thing that could have happened, because it did.

CHARLIE: Couldn't get it up?

ME: Bingo!

CHARLIE: Did it happen eventually or one try and that was that?

ME: One try. I'm cursed.

CHARLIE: Then what—did you go home?

ME: No spent the night.

CHARLIE: Shouldn't be that big of a deal. Was she cool?

ME: I think she was disappointed.

CHARLIE: Any idea when you will see her again?

ME: This weekend.

CHARLIE: So no sweat. Make up for it with round two.

ME: What if I can't? It is bumming me out.

CHARLIE: Handle that ass. Don't doubt yourself. If you're that worried lay off on jerking off for a minute.

ME: Whatever, see you at the hookah spot.

Nothing will be original again. That might be the motto of the twenty-first century. Not "Know Thyself" engraved in gold letters above the entrance to a Delphic temple, but rather on the archway into an empty public pool in Brooklyn where summer concerts are held, written in a font meant to capture the nostalgia of handwriting: "Nothing will be original again." On the first date I disclosed everything: my ex-wife had an affair, I was a recovering alcoholic, I was estranged from my mother. I sabotaged myself, while simultaneously providing an exit strategy. The next day, I sent a two-page email. I didn't understand the rules. Wait two days to text back, three days to email, a week before IM-ing: "It was nice hanging out." The sad fact was I dated anyone for three weeks, committed all my attention and affection, out of romantic desperation meant to reinforce my own self-worth. I placed a doodle of a bird and a heart on her pillow as I left for work. I called the next day, maybe twice. I didn't want to be alone. I needed to set clearer boundaries for myself. What is the appropriate timeline to feel something like love again? *I'm supposed to feel consumed. It happens like a thunderbolt or a fork in a socket.*

I couldn't help but envision how each person had rested their hand on a chest not so unlike mine, watched their favorite movie on this couch at night, months before, with someone else. There are too many people in the world, and sitting in front of a screen exchanging messages and staring at photos creates desire and boundless possibilities. Once face-to-face in reality, it's not so much that expectations are tarnished, but that there was a fear of missing out on the host of other options. But more importantly for me, it was as if my own individuality, if there is such a thing, felt insignificant, felt routine, felt like a bit part played night after night onstage. I don't have any way to say it without feeling like Bridget Jones; I wanted it to be distinct with me. And yet what if history was doomed to repeat itself, like the sad man living in the desert struck by lightning four or five times in a life? The lightning's electric charges lingering within said man's circulatory system like a parasite, defying the laws of science and recruiting future bolts of lightning from the sky to strike the body again, and then again, and then for good measure once again, not delivering love, but burns, disfigurement. I wanted to believe my luck at finding someone was neutral—my odds the same as my peers—the customary 50/50 chance of success. Heads or tails. It is the law of probability. Each time we begin again with renewed optimism or faith in our luck. The alternative is too depressing to maintain.

Throughout it all I wouldn't let myself forget that on the rare occasions in my marriage when I did have sex with Nina, she was also having sex with someone else. Thinking of him as she was with me, coming home after she was with him, or going off to see him after she was with me, each time returning to play out a domestic routine I believed to be scripted only for us. Sam asked me if I still thought about her. He told me he did as well, that he missed her too, and I knew it was important that he tell me that. After a half a year without her, he was the first one to say that to me. It was easier each day for me to write her off. I'd become accustomed to such a position with people. It was my life's work. I didn't tell him that I had recently found her Social Security card in a stack of random papers. I brought it to work to shred before thinking better of it and mailing it to her mother in a package of other miscellaneous documents.

September 5, 2007
Dear Sophie,

I apologize for emailing you, particularly at your work address, and hope it is not too much of an inconvenience. Really, I just wanted to write to let you know that I do appreciate your calling me and providing me with information I undoubtedly deserved to know. I have since left the Bay Area and moved back to Brooklyn. I hope all is as well with you as it could be.

All best,
Brett

※

Sophie Reynolds's reply was generous, kind, and sympathetic. She was relieved to know how I felt, that I didn't hold *The Phone Call* against her. We were sharing a trauma, attempting to make sense of our pasts and finding support in our friends. We were alone in the world together, distinctly undergoing a similar range of emotions—the predicament of infidelity by no means unique to us, except that regardless of our separate lives we had somehow become characters in the same drama.

After posting that first fake Missed Connection, I convinced Jess to write some more with me. It became slightly obsessive. I was posting one or two a day. Craigslist had begun "ghosting" my posts—meaning they were published, but not included publicly in the queue. To get around this, I had to post from different computers with new IP addresses, using different email addresses that I had to create weekly. If I was at a friend's for dinner, I retired to their office to post from their computer. It wasn't quite cloak-and-dagger, but I allowed myself to entertain the idea that it was.

I found it didn't really matter what I posted. Responses would flood in almost immediately:

> I look every day, wondering if someone feels like I got away :)
> Oh well . . . we can't all be the "cute hipster girl reading *Pride and Prejudice and Zombies* on the G train." But sometimes I'd like to think when I catch a guy stealing glances that the universe is setting up a moment that will ensure that I will stick in his mind for at least an hour ;) I read missed connections too, for entertainment, and for the slim chance someone spotted me on the train and thought I was the most beautiful thing in the world. They are like little love stories. I reconnected with someone on here that I spoke to once, because I too looked to kill time at work. I thought I would go for it—the one written about me. The guy ended up being tragically boring. What a cliché. Romance is dead. LOL. I still read them.

Jess and I emailed back and forth during work hours, sometimes writing just a phrase, sometimes a full sentence or two, the other person adding on from there, and then I posted them to Craigslist.

SUBJECT: L Train this Morning / m4w / Brooklyn

You were on the L train wearing skinny jeans and an expression of doubt. I share that doubt, and wanted to share my thoughts on podcasting, 19th century Russian novels, and French pressed coffee. Your body language implied you are interested in these things, as well as polka music (in a strangely unironic way), East Asian horticulture, and car racing. I could tell that you were listening to some minimal techno, or electro, or Silver Jews, or Jigga. And so was I. I think that if we meet, I will explode into knowing the exact way to sing in the shower and cook pasta for your tiny mouth. If you felt the same way, let me know, smoke signals, etc.

I waited. Smoked a cigarette. I refreshed my inbox. A reply:

I'll bet you enjoy the *Times* on Sunday, spending your weekends lounging on a blanket at McCarren Park playing Scrabble
after a large brunch. If you'd like to, we can watch independent
films, cook dinner listening to 60s Motown records and you
can marvel at my random use of antiquated diction and perfect
spelling.

And another:

What color were the jeans and what time was it? I'd hate to
be the wrong person to converse with about polka music over
pasta . . .

I searched *The New York Times* for articles about online dating and found "Looking for Love: Online or on Paper," in which the author noted that in 1841 a German aristocrat, Baron von Hallberg de Bröch, placed a full-page ad in the *Journal of Munich* boasting of a sumptuous castle and received seven hundred letters in response. Among the qualifications the seventy-year-old baron required in his prospective partner: "She must be from sixteen to twenty years of age; she must have beautiful hair, handsome teeth, and a charming little foot." Where were my seven hundred emails?

I refreshed my inbox:

> I was sitting on the L train this morning though I'm positive
> your missed connection was not with me. I can't help but want
> something big to happen soon. Like really soon. Like in twenty
> minutes soon. When the class is over soon. I hate Wednesdays
> and expectations always harm more then they help. Maybe one
> day I'll inspire a random show of affection in the form of a
> shower bravado and pasta cooking . . .

And

> Quite possibly could have been me. I make coffee for a living. I
> prefer clover pressed. Am I yours?

I refilled my coffee. I looked up "clover pressed." I learned that
the final step, "when a cake of spent grounds rises majestically
to the top, is so titillating to coffee fanatics that one of them
posted a clip of it on YouTube." I watched the video on YouTube.
I refreshed my inbox:

> I'm not your lady, but I hope some kind of poetic justice is
> served in that you and your lady will be sharing a cup of French
> pressed coffee in no time. Possibly even each of you having a
> cup of your own. Good luck.

I felt awful. I emailed Jess and told her I was awful. She wrote back: "Maybe you are filling the world with hope rather than toying with it." I fancied myself the perfect flâneur, as described by Baudelaire, though instead of strolling the physical avenues and arcades of the modern city of Paris, I was idling my time away taking in the personal ads of the Internet. The flâneur, according to Baudelaire, has the unique ability to set up home everywhere in the world; "being at the center of the world and remaining hidden in the world," he experiences "some of the smallest pleasures of those independent minds, passionate, impartial, that language can only clumsily define. The observer is a prince who rejoices in all his incognito."

But that was just a theory to tell myself. In fact, it was more like I was trolling the universe. Though I never did write back or engage beyond the initial posting, I wasn't an observer. I was inserting myself into the activity of the passing multitude. I believed, for the most part, the majority of people reading the posts were somehow consciously or unconsciously in on the joke, that in the end the Missed Connection post itself was the point, was the event they were responding to. The joy was in knowing that others were out there, passing strangers, just like me, secretly hoping, quietly looking.

*

Someone responded:

That might be one of the best Missed Connections ever, you made my day.

After dating online for several months, I was caught off-guard out on a second date when the girl mentioned a specific life detail I hadn't yet confessed: "Didn't you meet your ex-wife at a pencil factory?" I changed the subject, made a lame joke about erasing a rough draft. I was positive it wasn't something I had shared. In fact, I had forgotten that detail entirely. At home, I searched my emails for confirmation. Nothing. I googled myself. The first result to appear, after .15 seconds, was my wedding announcement in *The New York Observer*. *Fuck the Internet*.

NINA AND BRETT
MET: September 2001
ENGAGED: December 13, 2003
PROJECTED WEDDING DATE: May 21, 2005

The two bards first met back at a party in Williamsburg held in an abandoned pencil factory. The long-haired Brett was wearing big Gucci sunglasses with clear lenses. "I knew who Brett was, but I had never formally met him," said Nina, 25, a tall brunette. "I was watching him all night. He was leaning against a wall, smoking, and just looked mysterious and cool." When Marvin Gaye's "Let's Get It On" started playing, she walked up to Brett and asked him to dance. "He turned around, looked at me and said no," Nina remembered. "I thought, O.K., so he's a jerk."

"I was shocked!" protested Brett, 26 (and no relation to Matt Lauer). "I was on my way out and saying goodbye to people, and this person who I had noticed earlier in the night to be quite beautiful approached me. I remember going home and asking my roommate if I should go back to the party."

Luckily, the circle of young poets in New York City is quite small and several weeks later Brett got word of a publication party for a magazine Nina publishes in her spare time. "I was sort of waiting for the right time to talk to her again," he said. "My temperament is not the kind that I could have contacted her and said, 'Hey, remember that time you asked me to dance?'" He missed the party, but sent her an e-mail requesting a copy, which she delivered at a subsequent reading held by his office. The scribes then made plans for a hipster pilgrimage to an art exhibit at P.S. 1 in Queens. Sitting in a small room with a Janet Cardiff installation involving choral music playing through speakers, Nina realized that she had stumbled into something big. "It was so beautiful, and I think we ended up just sort of staring at each other," she said. "It had this very personal and intimate feel to it," Brett recalled.

Yet their first kiss didn't come until almost two months later. "Nina took the lead on that one," Brett sighed, who rallied by buying her a recording of the aforementioned choral music for Valentine's Day. Nina explained that she "knew right away that he was it."

The couple picked out an antique 18-carat filigreed gold band with a small flat diamond set in the center, from Doyle and Doyle on Orchard Street. "I wanted a ring that looked like my mom's," said Nina. When the crucial moment arrived, Brett gallantly tried to drop to his knee, but Nina stopped him. "I freaked out," she said. "I didn't want to be looking down at him. So I made him stand up. He asked me to marry him, and then we sat down and stared at each other like morons."

There were rules to my new world order. It is safe to assume that each active participant on a dating site has at least three queries out at a time. People say things like dating is a numbers game, a game of chance, but also implied is that the more people one dates or meets (think speed dating), the better their odds are in encountering someone who is bearable. It's also about timing: Mercury is in retrograde, I'm not quite over my last lover, I had a bad day at work and wasn't in the mood for sushi.

A month had passed when Lindsay emailed me again. We had exchanged a few emails on the dating site and then silence—she disappeared. It happens. Lindsay's email didn't explain much, she was traveling, she was sorry so much time had passed since her last email—it would be reasonable to assume she had been dating someone else or trying to date someone else, just as I was. Lindsay's timing wasn't exactly great; I was reading the email at the end of my workday, right before heading out of the office to meet a date in the Lower East Side for tea. Or actually, maybe it was perfect timing.

September 7, 2007
Lindsay!

Oh you don't need to worry about blowing me off, leaving me out in the cold, high and dry; you just owe me for all the tissues I wadded up with tears and the pints and pints of ice cream I consumed in sadness. It is nice to hear from you, though of course, I have met my Internet life partner, actually all lucky thirteen of them.

If you can believe it, I haven't and am emailing you on a Friday night. I should have waited until morning. Anyway, now, I have a strange-ish question: Were you by any chance at Teany tonight?

Here I am,
Brett

※

And, small as the real world can be, it was in fact Lindsay sitting five feet from me, hours after she sent her email, and an hour into my awkward first date with someone else.

September 8, 2007
Dear Lindsay,

It goes without saying that it was incredibly weird. And I was sitting there thinking why is this pretty girl smiling at me, that never happens, am I going to have to look at Craigslist Missed Connections or something, and then a split second later, I though OH, maybe . . . I admit though I'm happy we got the awkwardness of our first date over with. It was a demo. And I'm not quite sure that I was out on a date last night, but I will roll with that since it was a person who contacted me from my profile, but she lives in Boston, and was in town and wanted to meet, and so I thought, eh, whatever. When I described her "accent" to a friend, he informed me that "weally" isn't a Boston accent, but a speech impediment. So, I can promise there was no hand-holding. I can also promise my favorite color is blue, that I like birds, and just got a manicure. And where will you be for the weekend?

Soon,
Brett

PS: I had my intern at work crunch some numbers today as to the probability (in percentages) of an encounter at a tea shop in the Lower East Side.

See attached file.

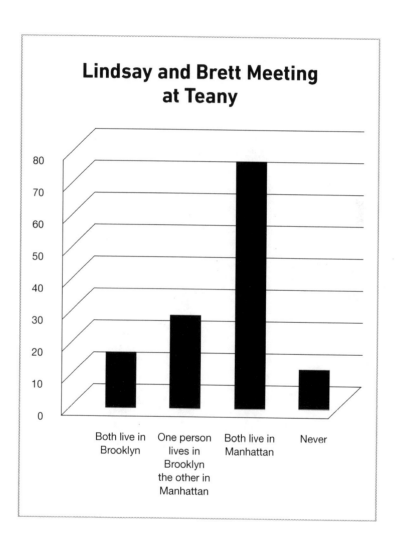

Lindsay and Brett Meeting at Teany

Both live in Brooklyn | One person lives in Brooklyn the other in Manhattan | Both live in Manhattan | Never

We traded a few more emails, and then for whatever reason, laziness or life intervened, and a week passed without my responding. Late one night an angry and indignant email arrived from Lindsay. Among other things, it questioned my basic decency and offered the advice that I refrain from acting like an asshole, if not for her sake, then for the sake of all my potential future dates. It would save everyone a good deal of time, waiting, suffering, and expectation. She wasn't exactly right, but also, maybe she wasn't wrong, and it was certainly the opportunity for me to bow out gracelessly. I will say, though, her email was funny, well-written, and full of passion, and I'd become recently accustomed to apologizing for performing incorrectly, knowingly or unknowingly. And so, I didn't move on to someone else and instead sent an apology and made plans to meet in person.

October 11, 2007
Lindsay,

I'm sorry to receive your email and did have every intention of emailing you back and while I could list reasons (from an insane and draining work week to my own recent dating experiences and taking a few days before leaping back in) they are still not adequate, as I'm not dead, and there have been no deaths in my immediate family and so I should have emailed you. And I do sincerely apologize for that. I couldn't agree more that dating is exhausting and perhaps a little disheartening and I certainly had no intentions of exasperating you.

Having said all that, I can't help but think that your email is a little misdirected. We didn't date or even really meet; we exchanged a bunch of emails that I really looked forward to receiving and there was certainly the expectation of meeting. So maybe "unstoppable moron" might be a little much? You took over a month to respond to me and I don't think you should be so quick to hold others to a standard which you yourself are unable or unwilling to live up to. I was disappointed when you didn't email me, but I certainly would not judge you so harshly because of it.

And still don't,
Brett

My friend Charlie and I constantly found ourselves at the hookah spot. The walls were painted with a form of hieroglyphics. It was as if the person hired had recreated the symbols from the memory of a half-hour school lesson on ancient Egypt rather than modeling them on actual images, or as if strict copyright laws required each hieroglyph to be altered 30 percent to avoid a lawsuit. The lights were dimmed and that helped. We sat on fringed cushions and ordered cherry mint tobacco and mint teas. We were both single and we both didn't drink, so late in the evening, after a movie, instead of ending up at a bar, we found ourselves there. On Wednesday nights a DJ played Top 40 hip-hop and R&B, on Thursdays it was filled with drag queens performing lap dances for middle-aged men, and on Friday nights it was filled with teenage ravers. All the waitresses were young women from former Soviet countries. The place wasn't going to last but it was three blocks from Charlie's apartment.

I sat with the long hookah hose in my hand puffing scented tobacco. We handed it back and forth. We looked at our phones and talked about girls and my online dating. I told him how someone had emailed me who recognized me from an Oakland coffee shop, that I exchanged emails with her about the differences between Brooklyn and the Bay Area. She lived ten blocks down the street from me. We IMed each other for a month or so, she sent me a mixed CD of moody songs, and we never met. I told him about how Daphne still wouldn't let me completely end our relationship, though I wasn't exactly standing my ground either. One morning before work, we were on the roof of her apartment building smoking, and ended up having sex on plastic patio furniture. We stopped when the condom broke. I called a pharmacy near my work to find out if they sold the morning-after pill. We rode the subway for twenty minutes in silence. At the pharmacy, as I pulled out my wallet to pay, a strip of three condoms fell onto the counter. Daphne had slipped them into my pants when

I was in the shower as a joke. I told Charlie how, on the way to meet him, I received three text messages. One from Bella, asking if I wanted to go to a concert; one from Christine asking why I wouldn't text her back; and one from Lindsay asking for a picture of my penis.

We looked at our phones and browsed online profiles. I had signed up for the dating site at the standard free membership level, but recently upgraded to Gold Status for $34.94 a month. A date told me she thought I must be "loaded" because I had paid the premium fees, while at the same time wondering how pathetic a person must be to splurge for the Gold Status. But now I had such benefits as: "Show up at the very TOP in searches; Be the FIRST to contact new members; Get FULL access to members' recorded video intros; FULL access to blogs and group features; and most importantly, Access to EXTRA LARGE photos." We looked at the extra-large photos and we noticed there were trending similarities for the women I clicked on. These women liked a night out, but also, a night in watching movies; travel; someone who felt comfortable in a suit, but also looked good in a T-shirt and Converse. A surprising number of women listed *Secretary* as their favorite movie. Or rather, the women whose profile pictures resulted in a click of my mouse tended, overwhelmingly, to list *Secretary* as their favorite movie. We were trying to find the next person I would wink at or hot-list.

We watched videos online related to the book *The Game*, mostly as a joke, but I couldn't help waiting for some secret to be revealed. We passed the hookah hose back and forth. The videos were a series of informational demonstrations on how to "neg" a girl—to use a mild insult meant to shift the power from her to you and capitalize on her insecurity. There was the technique of feigning interest in a prospective mark's friend, presenting a nonthreatening personality while also creating a spirit of competition between two women; or using an opener like: "My friend and I were taking a poll, do you floss after you brush your teeth or before?" Something, anything different to distinguish yourself from others, even creating a larger-than-life personality by "pea-cocking." Wear a top hat. Wear a gold dookie chain with a tiger pendant. I devised my own opener: "I was just talking with my friend and we can't remember: Did Kevin and Winnie ever finally date on *The Wonder Years*?"

I told Charlie that the antidepressants my doctor had pre-scribed made it difficult for me to reach climax, and that my doctor had tried a variety of cocktails to offset the side-effect (half a Wellbutrin and a whole Lexapro, skip taking my pill on the weekends I had planned a date). I finally just gave up and tried to turn it into a positive—I could last forever! One woman told me that I "fucked like a girl." I asked her if she meant it was difficult for some women to reach climax during sex. I felt proud to have a window into the female experience. She clarified by saying, "You never just jack-hammer me like a man."

Somehow even after her less-than-gentle reproach proclaiming I was a moron, I had been dating Lindsay for a month, by which I mean she was making the trek to my apartment in the evenings to binge-watch *Veronica Mars* and spend the night. Questions about the status and nature of the relationship became part of the conversation. I could say I still hadn't adequately absorbed proper dating etiquette, but that would be disingenuous, and yet, knowing better, I ended the relationship via email.

Lindsay responded and let me know, in summary, that I could go fuck myself. I deleted my part of the correspondence and forwarded Lindsay's email to a few close friends. I had come to think of it as my civic duty to keep them up-to-date on the breaking news of my post-marriage Internet dating life, to provide amusing rubbernecking at the wreck I managed to make. The majority of my friends were married, had been married long before the popularity of Internet dating. I had been in long-term relationships since all my friends had known me, and thus they had no context for this version of me meeting potentially amorous strangers. Dating and talking about dating had come to consume my life. I had moved through the various stages of grieving to arrive somewhere on the border between depression and acceptance. These dating stories, at the very least, were good brunch conversation, but also—my friends had hope for me. They believed my failures would eventually pass, that there was a pinhole of grayish light and fog becoming visible at the end of the tunnel, revealing a girlfriend I would feel comfortable enough to bring to brunch and introduce in person.

But after sending Lindsay's email to my friends, I might have regretted it. I began to see her email not necessarily as a case study for my overall dating conduct, or the definitive evidence to corroborate my failings, but as a pretty damning indictment. In part, this was a result of having shared her words with friends. They were no longer private—they were a narrative I felt I was required to defend, to articulate why and how this person could harbor such hostility toward me. Her email wasn't just expressing a desire for me to die in the most gruesome and horrible ways, but contained pointed words. She noted that, at the very least, she expected to receive some poetic words while dating a poet, and she should have known it was a bad omen that I never provided her with any. She wasn't misguided to expect appropriate gestures, even of the false variety. When I was sixteen and required to write a few sentences about poetry, I proclaimed: "Poetry is communication, and what on this planet is more important than that? Communication saves marriages, stops wars, and keeps the heart beating." I certainly thought poetry's value was in its attempt to communicate something that had the potential to alter the course of events, that it was the pure expression of truth and emotion. But almost twenty years had passed, and that feeling had degraded, or mutated, or modulated into a feeling of estrangement, disconnection, and helplessness at attempting to communicate anything, through poetry or otherwise.

All we are given during the initial dating period are such small signs, omens of future behavior: how our prospective partner tips the waiter, if they walk you to your subway station or hail a cab, if they smile back at a toddler on the street, or if there is aluminum foil on the ceiling of their apartment in order to prevent alien communication from penetrating their inner sanctum. It is always the small things. All I could provide for Lindsay, or anyone I dated, was the illusion that she could understand me. I supplied the plot points for each woman to construct her own narrative, rather than expressing my own.

Certain things were taken for granted: our stances on abortion; the importance of art and culture; we would of course vote Democrat; but the surface hid everything beneath, and the illusion on her part was that I would share those depths with her. Lindsay, for one, had believed whatever data was presented before the poet's eyes would be transformed into an emblem of feeling and an exclamation ending with an exclamation point! Instead, I had sat across from her in silence as she talked to me. The clock ticked slowly in the intervals it had perfected and we looked up at its face when there was a pause in the conversation.

Her email stung, and stung more once I had shared it with my friends who might have held better opinions of me. She didn't spare any four-letter expletives or cruel words in explaining that when we watched the documentary *The Bridge* and I didn't even hold her hand, that I was in essence an unfeeling monster. What

Lindsay was remarking on wasn't just my aloofness regarding commitment, but rather almost a model of withholding that couldn't be explained away as reservation or shyness. It suggested a cold indifference and cruelty. And furthermore, she was more prone to expect an openness and expressivity because I was a "poet." If indeed one spends his time thinking and attempting to articulate some strangeness in the world, it could be assumed that said person might extend such thought and care toward the person he is sleeping with, might wear his emotions on his sleeve like a blue flower, and share his overwhelming feelings about the world, love, the bare trees framed out the window, the songbirds in those trees singing as we drank coffee in bed on Sunday morning.

Instead, my impulse was to provide a smokescreen of facts as a version of sincerity. It was easier to say that my wife had an affair, and I was devastated, and leave it at that, than to begin the unpacking in a game of armchair therapy. It was easier to say I didn't speak with my mother than to discuss the ins and outs of childhood. Instead, I blew smoke out the window and summarized an article I just read, said things like: "Children of divorced parents divorce at a much higher rate, continuing the divorce cycle, the transmission of some cultural genetics, and so half of us are walking around with the mantra that we will not repeat the mistakes of our parents." I sat across from Lindsay, in silence, or she talked. Sure, I could have presented her with my daily inner monologue tentatively spoken aloud, watching her face for a reaction—some twitch, or raised eyebrow, or nod of recognition indicating we had stumbled onto some shared values. It would have been easier to lay a limp hand on hers as we watched a documentary showing footage of another body throwing itself off of the Golden Gate Bridge than to begin a conversation in which I expressed my sympathy with and desire to toss my own body off a bridge. Press repeat: *I am divorced, I am a recovering alcoholic, and by the fact of confessing such personal details, I have shared with you.* And perhaps we would have gotten to know each other over time through our working theories of the world. She'd learn to understand and appreciate mine and vice versa. But it was a bad sign I wasn't going to take the leap of faith beyond that.

I remained in touch with the many of the women I had dated. I'm not sure why, except that it required virtually no effort. I'm certain it was the same for them. We had friended each other on Facebook and there they were in my feed, or there they were a green dot in my Gchat contact list. I wanted to believe I displayed the comportment of an adult who had conducted himself properly, that sometimes things don't work out, and every instance of that is not a reflection of my poor behavior. There we were, still friends, though they had probably muted my posts. And yet, on the other end of the spectrum, sometimes that lack of a decisive and clean break led me to Bushwick or the East Village to spend the night with an ex long after we were in the habit of spending the night together. But in most cases, the connection I shared with my exes was a pretense of manners. I didn't really know the details of their lives, names of their family members, their particular tics and habits, and in fact we had made an active decision not to extend the effort to get know each other better. When we did chat, we were stuck with the limited shared subject matter—our time together—which meant rehashing that time, and how our respective dating lives had progressed.

March 18, 2008
9:38 PM

BELLA: Hello.

ME: You are always online these days.

BELLA: You know, I'm just here to see how your life is going to keep me awake in the wash of boredom and bad office lighting.

ME: That makes me sad. Should I send you emails to keep you updated?

BELLA: Actually, I really just want to know about the cats. Can you send me hourly reports on their movements?

ME: I gave my kittens to the Salvation Army to help with missionary work.

BELLA: What noble creatures.

ME: They are in Darfur right now.

BELLA: How selfless of them. But seriously, how is your life these days?

ME: You know, it is just kind of average.

BELLA: Details?

ME: What do you want to know? I cry myself to sleep. Stuff like that.

BELLA: Like, cry yourself to sleep after you have sex with lots of different women?

ME: T O N S. No, nerd.

BELLA: But some women, right?

ME: That is what us boys do.

BELLA: It seems like it. Like everyone wants to see lots of other people.

ME: Do you mean people want to see other people AND you?

BELLA: I guess. I just pin a lot of hope on these dates because they seem special and then I feel used when nothing comes of them.

ME: But you felt that I used you, or that you wasted your time with me?

BELLA: Yeah, like I invested more time in what was happening and then it was over.

ME: But dating is set up that way.

BELLA: Maybe that's the problem. I have too many.

ME: Too many what? How many dates do you go on?

BELLA: One a night.

ME: Really? You tramp, I thought I was special.

BELLA: You were special.

ME: Um, so were you.

BELLA: Then why did you keep your profile active?

ME: I just never ever signed out.

BELLA: Why do you think it didn't work out with us?

ME: Why do you think other girls didn't work out? I didn't want to commit.

BELLA: That makes me sad.

ME: Sad why?

BELLA: Sad that you go out on all these dates knowing before-hand that even if it's an amazing girl and an amazing date, in the end, it will end.

ME: Isn't that what people do?

BELLA: All people don't screw over other people.

ME: I haven't. Look who is talking.

BELLA: All people don't assume a relationship's end from the beginning. That is not what I call a real relationship.

ME: What else is there?

BELLA: There are people who stop looking at other potential girls for a whole week when they start seeing someone they might end up liking. Why do you check emails from strangers when you're with someone who isn't one? Why would anyone do that?

ME: Because it is there. Because someone has emailed them. Because they might have had other emails in the works.

BELLA: It's not just there. It's there because you set up a profile and asked it to be there.

ME: It is there. It is like checking email or something. It doesn't even really mean anything.

BELLA: Do you think that all men think this way? Or that it's fair to ask a guy to shut down his profile if I'm seeing him for a few months?

ME: I don't think there is anything wrong with asking that and doing that, but if it is there then they will look.

BELLA: I don't understand men, I guess.

ME: I am useless with providing insight into the male psyche.

BELLA: This is seriously keeping me up at night and not in a good way. My not understanding. It makes me want to give up dating for good.

ME: Then give up.

BELLA: Or maybe I could go back a decade and meet a guy at a bar or through friends.

ME: But let's also think this through a second, what would the equivalent be in a more traditional setting? You go on one or two dates with someone. Do you ask them to stop flirting with other people?

BELLA: What's your point?

ME: I'm brainstorming. At what point does someone ask for exclusivity?

BELLA: I guess when you've been dating for a while and it seems like the relationship could get more serious while still being fun.

ME: That is what is weird about online dating, it speeds everything up and one gets the feeling that they know a person really well.

BELLA: If you were seeing someone and started to feel like you knew that person well, would you close down your profile?

ME: I guess. I don't keep looking, not when I am seeing someone.

BELLA: But you didn't feel like you were seeing me.

ME: I didn't really, and that was because the whole thing was new and it was more from curiosity and more to make me feel like I was cute or interesting after having that taken from me from my marriage.

BELLA: Do you think I'm being needy or mean?

ME: I don't think you are. And I can take it.

BELLA: So what if when people start dating, they take it slow?

ME: If you saw a person once a week getting to know them it might be different. It is also a little about taking a risk or a leap of faith in a person, but that makes you vulnerable.

BELLA: Is it silly that I want someone to take a risk with me? To think it was worth it to be vulnerable for me?

ME: I don't think that is silly at all.

BELLA: I feel like we get each other. We get along well. Why can't we just hang out?

ME: Ask me to do something, we can hang out, we can go see a movie, but you can't hold my hand. I have been lucky in meeting people who are interesting and smart. I mean everyone I have spent time with I would still want to be in touch with. I like them all.

BELLA: But even if you're with a great person, you end it.

ME: Yes. Something just ended today!

BELLA: Why did it end?

ME: Why do you think?

BELLA: Ok, fine.

ME: Fine what?

BELLA: Fine, I get it, you don't want to commit to anyone, no matter how perfect, no matter how much that sucks—there is no person on earth you would commit to right now.

ME: I don't feel like I am ready, but don't want to be alone with my cats watching *Law & Order* either. Or maybe I do.

BELLA: I just ended something too.

ME: How long did you see them for?

BELLA: A few weeks.

ME: Why am I a little jealous?

BELLA: Because you have a little soul left. It actually sucks, the breakup I mean.

ME: I'm sorry that didn't work out. What was his problem?

BELLA: He didn't have a problem.

ME: I mean what did he say?

BELLA: He said that he needed more from me, sexually.

ME: Did you write him and tell him that was shitty?

BELLA: No.

ME: But you slept with him?

BELLA: No. Does that make what he said ok?

ME: I think that is understandable, sometimes people need intimacy, so can you just chalk it up to that, or is that such a guy thing?

BELLA: It is a guy thing.

ME: Yeah, you are such a girl.

BELLA: I feel bad because I actually liked him. I feel cheap, emotionally cheap.

ME: Don't feel cheap. You let your guard down and were vulnerable and the person wasn't right.

BELLA: It just feels raw.

ME: How recent is this?

BELLA: This week.

11:37 PM

BELLA: Why did you hook up with me if you knew you weren't going to keep seeing me?

ME: I didn't know that then. That is something I am figuring out.

BELLA: It just seems like you knew your state of mind well enough to know that people could get hurt. You said you wanted more intimacy and then you said you weren't ready for it.

ME: I'm not sure I know what you are getting at. I didn't know those things when I was seeing you. I knew I liked you, but I was worried that you were one of the first people I dated, and didn't have a handle on what I thought about dating. I said that about more intimacy, because I did want that, and was hurt when you blew me off, but I knew why, and thought you were acting reasonable.

BELLA: I guess.

ME: I don't know. The other thing might be that I get close enough to people in a certain space of time and then realize whoa, I like this person but don't love this person, and so then break it off. I don't know. I have no grand theories. I try the best I can.

BELLA: Did you have sex with the other girls you dated?

ME: Why would you need to know that?

BELLA: Just wondering.

ME: Yes.

BELLA: Maybe that is why they fell for you.

ME: In each case, I tried to say that wasn't important and that we shouldn't have sex, which is apparently a foolproof way to have sex. But also, I think you are giving my sexual prowess too much credit.

BELLA: Oh, so you have your tricks to get girls to have sex with you? Sex can actually be a big deal.

ME: I was kidding. And I know it is, and was one of the reasons I was trying to delay it.

BELLA: It is really good we didn't do anything.

Maybe every woman dating a poet deserves to have him tell her flowery things. Even given my complicated indifference to dating, it was strange I didn't write an ode to anyone's eyes, breasts, or particular gait. Lord knows I had nothing else to do and I've written poems from less, from assignments from professors restricted to the lexicon found in the business section of *The New York Times*. I could have said something. And it wouldn't be much of a lie to say that is how, in fact, I came to write poetry in the first place—from a wooing derived from lust.

I was in elementary school when I wrote my first poem for a classmate, but before I wrote poetry I pretended to write poetry. I don't mean this as an aesthetic or qualitative judgment, but rather as fact; I declared something written by another as my own. Really, it only happened once, in fourth grade. I handed Carolyn a note about how it would be pleasant if I could caress her body, because unlike a lot of girls, she had an especially nice one, but even still I should have had second thoughts before I just simply handed my heart over to her.

I was an eleven-year-old boy in pegged stonewashed jeans, and I was certain these direct and heartfelt verses would woo my crush—just as a twenty-four-year-old pop sensation with frosted hair, a dangling cross earring, and eternal sunglasses must have thought when he wrote them. They were, of course, the lyrics to George Michael's "Faith."

In my defense . . . actually, I'm not sure where to start. I could say I was young, overeager, and hadn't received a classroom lecture on the ethics of plagiarism. I could say it had been a difficult year—the year my parents' divorce became finalized. I don't want to rationalize my actions or be embarrassed to say George Michael's poetry spoke to me, but it did, and I am.

More importantly for this story, I was stuck with a staggering inability to speak with Carolyn in public. It was more than just generating the nerve to walk across the wood-chipped playground, from the jungle gym where I was positioned with a group of boys to where Carolyn stood each day near the seesaw with two or three other girls. I was sick with something, obsessed with a new-found bewilderment I was unable to articulate. I'm sure I didn't understand the relationship of boyfriend and girlfriend beyond the names assigned. Abstractly, I knew bodies touched, as in holding hands. So I listened to George Michael's album over and over in my living room. I put my headphones on. I turned up the volume. I felt the lyrics and emotions of the song were part of my own psyche, and I apparently came to the conclusion that there was no more perfect way to express my inner feelings than to transcribe the lyrics and address the note "for your eyes only."

I am sorry I didn't even quote lyrics to Lindsay, or Daphne, or Bella, to say "I was listening to this song, and thought of you," or at the very least write an acrostic poem constructed from the first letter of their names. It would have been painless for me to do, to conjure the muses for a bit of occasional verse—something I certainly had done for birthday cards for friends, even as a post on Facebook walls. All I can say is I wasn't ready. *Sadly, let me explain, let me try to tell you everything. All I can say is I wasn't ready to commit to a level of faith with you. Yes, everything I said was honest and true.* I could have used those for the last lines of Lindsay's acrostic. But I was already working on this document. I was compiling and rereading the emails from my marriage. I knew this story wanted to tell itself, and I knew deep in my heart Lindsay wouldn't be there for the end of it.

I can't remember when my father started dating again. I'm not sure what advice the self-help books have for single fathers, but they can't possibly dwell enough on the unnaturalness of a child waking up to his father making eggs for a woman in a robe who is not his mother. I think I was eleven.

What remains more potent, more available to the complex mechanisms and pathways in my brain, is the moment marking the end of my parents' marriage. They had been separated for years when my father told me it was official; he and my mother were getting divorced. We were driving home from a department store, and I was in the backseat—I'm not sure why, this was before families adopted such safety precautions—and I began to cry hysterically. The word itself was like a curse being cast. Enter the dark clouds, thunder, sinister howling from a black cauldron. Even if I knew that a divorce was a possibility, it was the first time one of my parents, not an older brother, was explaining it to me. It wasn't just the acknowledgement of a family unit splitting; it was that the people I had instinctively trusted as beyond reproach in their authority and wisdom, because they were my parents, because I simply didn't know any better or wouldn't let myself know better, even when I had witnessed their undeniable sadness and anger with each other, were failures. And as a child crying, hyperventilating and banging his chest with his fists in the backseat, "divorce" seemed to mean that, if the people who were given to me as models were failures, all failure was now possible. My uncontrollable outburst was reason enough for him to slip a note under my bedroom door after we had a fight. If email had existed, surely he would have emailed me from a laptop downstairs. I don't recall the particulars of the fight; all I have is his letter.

August 8, 1990
Brett,

Sometimes in conversation we bang heads . . . we don't really listen . . . even though we do understand. It is hard because we are both trying to look out for our own interests and they may not always match up with each other. Certainly what you said about Janet is correct . . . but times and situations have changed. You know that of course. In past years I could easily take you to the mall, soccer game, wrestling practice, art fair, you name it, because I had a partner to come home to. What crosses my mind now, and maybe it is somewhat unfair to you, but it's a fact nonetheless . . . in six years you'll be gone . . . college, work, who knows. If I don't establish some other relations or relationships, Brettski, I'm going to be alone. I don't like that thought. So here's what happens . . . I'm trying to develop a relationship with Janet. (I like her a lot . . . she's a nice person and already cares a lot about you guys.) At this point I can't predict what'll happen between the two of us, but I certainly don't want to lose you because of her. That is why I try to include you in many of the things we do. I like to share my experiences with people. You for one . . . and certainly Paul and Noah and Simon. I'm not trying to cut my time with you, I'm just trying to fit you in. Believe me she recognizes the awkwardness of the situation. She's a very sensitive lady. She is constantly on me to spend time with you guys and rightfully so. Many of the days she doesn't come over occur because she knows I want to spend time with you. Of course often you're out with your friends, but I do see you in passing, and can at least keep up with what is going on in your life. I like to know what you're doing, who you're hanging out with etc. I'm not nosey. I care about you. It would be nice if we could avoid the guilt trips, yelling, and cursing, but I guess that is going to be a part of our lives. As long as we know we love each other . . . I think we can always overlook and even laugh at the silly moments when we lash out at each other. There is certainly a lot of frustration in all of our lives right now. . . . I'm sure we'll work through it. Let's pull together. Talk if we can . . . write if we have to.

I love you very much,

Dad

Technically, I still wasn't divorced. It was some purgatory in-between stage like Dante's Belacqua waiting: "O brother, what's the use of climbing? / God's angel, he who guards the gate, would not / let me pass through to meet my punishment." The documents arrived on a Tuesday. Nina had addressed the envelope herself. What I had expected was different: a man in a tan suit would approach me and bum a cigarette. As he fumbled to light his cigarette he'd ask me to hold an envelope for a moment. Upon returning my lighter, the document still in my hand, he'd casually remark: "Mr. Lauer, you've been served." Then off he would walk down the road into the sunset. I don't believe this was an unreasonable expectation. I deserved a dramatic ending; I'd witnessed it countless times on television. Instead, in the top left-hand corner of an envelope, familiar cursive handwriting. Quite possibly, the last physical traces of Nina I would encounter. Of course I expected to be caught off-guard. I was caught off-guard. It was always the days when my mind was preoccupied, when I was in the middle of a conversation on the phone, balancing it between head and shoulder, that correspondence from her arrived. Never the day I paused, exhaled a breath, and turned the mailbox key.

The documents were just a template on white paper, the paragraphs of text a fading gray ink as if they had been previously Xeroxed a thousand times. Like the W-9's I sent out from my office. Some hand had touched them, though, as there was a blue checkmark in the box beside "Dissolution of the marriage based on," and then in a sub-box below, another blue checkmark beside: "irreconcilable differences." That's a phrase for you, a very simple umbrella phrase encompassing nearly everything. "She beat me." "He stole money from my parents." Really, anything. The familiarity of the phrase did provide a strange comfort. *Yes, I've heard that phrase before.* Every divorce is a series of stock phrases, actions, and emotions, but I wanted to leave a fucking paper trail of her deceit. I wanted it on public record. Irreconcilable differences.

It both articulates perfectly a series of events and feelings, and omits a particular brand of accountability from the official record. I spent two hours looking through files and transcribing income and expenses in duplicate. It was as if a coworker left a stack of work for me before going on a three-week cruise. I knew it wasn't rational, but I felt I shouldn't have to lift a finger for this divorce. It was her doing. I wanted it to be enough to say "Yes, it is over," but we had entered this contract legally, so we had to end it legally. Somewhere amongst all the boxes another was checked: "There are no minor children." That was what friends said. "At least you didn't have any kids." If for no other reason than that it expedited the process. I signed in duplicate. I paused before pressing the blue pen to each page, paused not from a feeling of uneasiness or mourning but from an obligation to note the moment without actually noting the moment. Maybe the pen wasn't blue. It doesn't matter; the documents were signed and sent to a government office building in Oakland. A period of time was legally required to pass. I waited. I waited some more.

4

It is true. I looked for Nina. I looked for her on the streets we had walked regularly, in the shops of our weekends, the restaurants we once frequented. In the distance any woman with long brown hair and bangs might be her, until after a time she was nowhere, or those places took on different meanings, or stores closed and were replaced with different stores.

At work, part of my day involved killing time—either as a result of boredom from repetitive office tasks such as stuffing envelopes, such as answering the phone, such as writing another email, or, on the other end of the spectrum, a respite required from the work stacked in neat piles on my desk, or rather simply, my boss was at a lunch meeting and the option to whittle time away presented itself. I read *The New York Times*, *Pitchfork*, friends' blogs, and friends-of-friends' blogs. And then I would find myself at my desk, watching the workday clock as the last hour of the day stuttered to conclusion, and place Nina's name in the search engine. It was what was expected of me. I want to say there was nothing special about it, that it wasn't loaded, that if I had work correspondence with someone living in Texas, I found myself doing the same for him as well. But the curiosity that drove this wonder was linked less with placing a face to a name and more about checking in on a wound. I wanted to know if her life had become "better" than mine, different than what she once envisioned for herself without me. But it also was no different than a changing of the seasons, an unpacking of my sweaters and scarves, placing them back under my bed, and preparing for what would come next. Mainly I searched for her name because I could, because it was there to be searched.

According to the Internet, Nina seemed to have embarked on a quiet and boring life of little digital relevance. Nothing came up. If she was on Facebook, she'd blocked me from accessing her account. I didn't blame her—I had blocked her from my page months ago. The majority of search results just spat back a list of the magazines and books we edited together, their availability now at a deep discount. The only images were the covers of the books themselves. No new information.

I went back to working, adding content to the workplace website, and after an hour of squinting at code, I posted what would be one of my last Missed Connections.

SUBJECT: Lorem Ipsum / m4w / 31 / New York

I'm placing this here for you. I will change it later.

Memories are forgotten with interference, when new objects of attention are placed in their pathways. Instead of looking for Nina—instead of looking at the morbid car crash on the side of the road—I looked the other way, across the grassy median and off into the distance. I signed in to the dating site. I hadn't seen "Croque Madame" before, hadn't sent any winks, and hadn't clicked the button adding her to my hot list. My user name was "The Emperor of Ice Cream," after the Stevens poem, and our two names sounded like a nice meal, a good date.

May 15, 2008
Dear Croque Madame,

That is a pretty funny username. But better yet, it led me to this: "Croque-monsieur's earliest published use has been traced back to volume 2 of Proust's *À la recherche du temps perdu* (191 . . . . . 🕸 ," which for some reason I think is amusing. Maybe that amusement is a result of a long and relatively unexciting work day. And your work day?

Yours,
Brett

In came one response to the Missed Connection:

Hey baby I'm here.

And then another:

Hey,

I'm working on a project about Missed Connections on Craigslist in NY and I was wondering if you would be willing to answer a few questions about your experience. I know that Craigslist is kind of sketchy to begin with and it's hard to trust anyone here, so we could talk via email and of course you could remain anonymous if you feel more comfortable this way. I am getting in touch with several people who post here so I could get a broad view on some of the issues I'm interested in. In general, this project will deal with the way people interact with each other, meet new people, and cope with loneliness; all in relation to living in New York.

I wanted to be done with it all. It wasn't just that the full-time job of posting Missed Connections had worn me down, that the creative impulse was waning, and that the thrill was gone, so to speak—all of which were true—but that the initial question of what would happen if I wrote and posted a fake Missed Connection had been answered. The responses had become invitations to someone else's bright idea for a project or dissertation, someone else's investigation into the art of loneliness. We come full circle to reporting on why any one of us is doing anything. And here I was, writing my own dummy text. *Lorem Ipsum*, the beginning of a block of Latin text used as placeholder text for graphic designers to return to later with the actual content of the design, the two words that begin it derived from a phrase meaning "pain itself." It had come to mean nothing, and yet was filled with the potential to be something, anything but itself. Here I was mourning my marriage, itself its own simulation of the outcome of a traditional connection and the failure of the supposed connection, so much so that a term was soon minted: starter marriage. Here I was having another coffee, half myself and half a version of who I thought would be desirable to the person sitting across from me. Here I was writing letters to my estranged mother, which I wouldn't send. I should have just been posting the letters to another section of the Craigslist bulletin board, Rants and Raves. Here I was placing the words one in front of the other, filling in my life's template until the real text was written and could be dropped into the design.

May 15, 2008
Dear Brett,

My work day has been uneventful. I work in the marketing department at a museum, and we're in a bit of a slow period in between
exhibitions at the moment. What do you do? I'm sitting here day-
dreaming about my weekend plans. Brunch will definitely figure
in. What are you up to this weekend?

Cheers,
Ingrid

May 15, 2008
Dear Ingrid,

Ok, and so emoticons are cool, and maybe I even use them every once and again etc. but, I don't know how that ended up in my last email. I work at the Poetry Institute as the Managing Director, and have been here for almost ten years now. I have the day off tomorrow to wait for a DSL service repair, conveniently any time between 8 AM and 7 PM. And then a friend is reading on Saturday, and maybe a little writing . . . but no big dreams.

B.

May 15, 2008
Dear Brett,

I enjoyed that little bespectacled emoticon! Even though it was obviously a mistake and made no sense. Poetry Institute? It's nice that you were able to actually find a job doing what you love! So rare. You have the WHOLE day off tomorrow? Granted, waiting around for a repair guy is the pits, but I'd love to laze around the house and watch daytime TV. Especially since it's going to be so rainy tomorrow.

Anyway, I have to run off to a work event. Ta for now!

Ingrid

P.S. This may be a little premature, but if you wanted to have a very low-pressure Sunday night drink, I could be up for that.

May 16, 2008
Dear Ingrid,

I would love to meet up for drinks on Sunday, but I don't drink, which isn't weird for me at all, but thought I should tell you. Maybe we could get coffee, tea, scones, play Boggle, something super high-pressure. Here is my email brettfletcherlauer@gmail .com if that is easier for you.

Hope your work event was fancy with cubes of cheese,

B.

Sometimes I looked at the Facebook pages of classmates from high school: puffy red faces, weight gained, and photos of newborns. Sometimes I googled myself and sometimes I googled my exes. I wanted to believe that elsewhere in the world, blocks from me, or somewhere in Middle America, in a moment of shared boredom, one of my exes sat at her desk engaging in the same pastime. I'd left them all a digital memoir, had been tagged by friends in embarrassing photos, posted my own photos in a horse's mask, in a rabbit's mask, posted an essay I'd written about online dating and Missed Connections. In one such workday search session, I was happy to discover the article announcing my engagement to Nina was finally on page four of search results for my name. Time moves on. According to the wisdom of the algorithm, which I can't pretend to understand though I've read the Wikipedia entry on it at least twice, I had been busy with more important things. It was during one of these googling sessions that I discovered Lindsay's blog.

I read the entire archive in one sitting and learned she was writing for a variety of comedy and pop culture websites, mostly recaps of *Glee* and *Parks and Recreation*. I also learned that she had started performing stand-up comedy. In the "About Me" section of her blog there was a list of upcoming dates where she could be found onstage. She'd been busy—when we were dating the requisite background search produced only records of the college clubs she'd participated in as an undergraduate. Among the various links on her blog, there was a link to a video of one of her shows.

It was the end of the day. I took out my headphones and plugged them into the computer speakers. I clicked the link. It looked like any stand-up club I'd seen on television: a person standing on a dark stage with a microphone, a brick wall in the background. Mostly her jokes were observational humor on dating and love; ridiculous things her mother said to her about her troubles finding Mr. Right. Midway through her bit on dating failures, she began a new bit on her Internet dating adventures. My palms started to sweat. I swiveled in my chair to take note of whether my coworkers were watching, if they had sidled up behind me and were now looking over my shoulder—as if the headphone cord had jerked loose and the audio found itself being broadcast for all to hear—to participate in wherever this setup was going.

She talked about being on the third date with a guy, and how the third date is traditionally the moment when people come clean, reveal something they were holding back, like when her date, says, "I have something I need to tell you," she is ready for anything: he has a kid, he killed a man in Reno to watch him die, his wife thinks she's cute. And it was funny; the way a person discussing with confidence what we might not reveal in the checkout line can be funny, and always more funny if you are sitting in the room with friends, preferably friends who have had a few drinks. The reveal—what the person disclosed on the third date, the date of intimate confession—was that he had witnessed a ghost in his apartment.

I paused the video, took off my headphones, went outside, and smoked a cigarette. I mentally replayed all our dates. We watched *The Bridge*, watched *Veronica Mars*, watched porn on my computer. I thought about how at the end of the relationship she kept texting me, once a month, always on the weekend, most often after midnight, and I would respond. *As long as she doesn't use my name. As long as she doesn't use my full name.* I smoked another cigarette.

I knew nothing was private anymore; everything was content, a story to retell as a blog post, a screenshot, a podcast, a stand-up routine, a memoir. This isn't exactly new. When you open yourself up to another person, or in my case just crack the door, a slim beam of sunlight shines through, and with or without the Internet you are subject to the possibility of humiliation, ridicule, or, at best, indifference. This brief video was allowing me to eavesdrop on the joke that was told about me at brunch the next morning. I was acutely aware of this from my own participation on the other end as storyteller, my inability to locate any higher moral ground to stand on. I had taken pains to present myself in a certain way to the world, and of course I had no power in how it was interpreted, particularly now, to an audience, to the hundreds of people who had watched the video. There was nowhere I saw this going that wouldn't humiliate me. I finished my third cigarette and walked slowly back to my office chair, head down, prepared for the shame I had coming. I put on my headphones.

It was funny; funnier in her telling, because she was animated, she was over-the-top, and so demanded the audience smirk and laugh with her. The big punch line wasn't so much a punch line, more a dramatic eye roll at how idiotic her date was, because, let's face it, people who see ghosts are the same people who see UFOs, who disbelieve the moon landing, or belong to the Flat Earth Society. And then it was also funny (again, in her retelling) because if the person telling her—me—actually did witness a spectral haunting, it means that said ghost was still lingering in the small apartment, hovering over the lovers, available at any moment for future appearances, such as, and not limited to, moments of lovemaking. So it was either ridiculous or spooky, maybe both. I wiped my palms on my jeans. Braced myself. I knew that this was just the lead-up, that a one-two punch was coming in which I would be thrown in front of the comedy train for maximum laughs. When the second hit didn't materialize and she moved on to other dates, other failures, I was relieved, possibly even grateful; I wanted to email "Thank you" but thought better of it—all emails lead to something else, further correspondence, more material— by then I knew not to commit anything to writing. What was written and sent, what was written and posted, became someone else's source material.

Dear Mom,

I fear in your private moments of contemplation at a copy machine at work, driving home, washing the dishes, that you have altered the version of events that have led me to my small desk, writing this letter I will not send. Memory does that, provides its own process of natural selection to ensure the survival of a species. I'm no different; each time I recall a memory I move on to something else. I light a cigarette, check my email. I try to forget.

"How dare he tell me not to drink," is what you told my brothers. I didn't tell you what you could or could not do. As god is my witness, I walked up after the wedding ceremony as you were ordering a glass of wine. I walked up without malicious intent. Noah was there. Let him testify, since later the story became: "He accosted me, he sabotaged me, he set me up." I asked you twice what you were doing; you kept your eyes on the wine list. "If you are going to drink, I'd prefer you leave." Such a tempered word, really, "prefer." To regard one more than another. I repeated myself. I repeat the events over and over. I've edited this down to a paragraph in order to not dwell too long on what can only be described as your willful obliviousness to the damage your alcoholism wreaked over the entirety of my childhood, spilling over into our present relationship. Since little will come from such accusations, I'll settle for calling what occurred simply a demonstration of bad manners. I can't help myself: that you would take my comments so lightly and disregard them at my wedding is staggering to me, and simultaneously a staggering testimony to the force of your addiction.

You told my brothers you didn't even want to go to the wedding, conjuring a false anger at the absence of a rehearsal dinner where you would have been provided the opportunity to meet my future in-laws and feel more comfortable. I understand this is traditional, but there was no rehearsal dinner because I was attempting to mediate your interactions with my father. Quite frankly, the anxiety of having two events at which something could go awry was a risk I wasn't willing to take. I had assumed there would be awkwardness for the group photographs, father on one side, and you on the other. I allowed for the possibility that you would utter some vicious words to my father or my step-mom as you found yourself accidentally waiting in line for the bathroom behind them. A snub. A "fuck you." This is what I had prepared myself to live with. But definitely not drinking. Some contracts I had thought were as good as spoken. The fact that you were there was an assumption you would not drink, was a condition I didn't actually foresee needing to be addressed. Some contracts are made with a general feeling of faith in right and wrong. Mom, I did not speak to you for those five years when I was a teenager because you were an alcoholic. I had experienced firsthand the effects of your alcoholism. This wasn't a secret.

Love,
Brett

May 17, 2008
1:44 PM

INGRID: So, did you enjoy snooping around my Facebook profile?

ME: Yes. I know too much now. I feel dirty.

INGRID: Ha! What? I hope you're joking.

ME: You aren't going to get much from mine.

INGRID: This totally gives you a leg up, conversationally.

ME: Do you need to know something? Like my favorite snack?

INGRID: No, I'm fine, but you can tell me if you'd like!

ME: Nah, I will keep it secret.

INGRID: Suspense!

ME: I'm a little surprised you didn't ask me about being divorced. That is always the first question.

INGRID: Oh, whatever. You can just tell me about that whenever you feel comfortable. It's not like you're asking me for my dating history right off the bat.

ME: Actually, if you could provide that . . .

INGRID: Ha! I'll tell you whatever you want to know, I'm an open book. I also have some amazing online dating disaster stories, if you're interested.

ME: I don't feel uncomfortable about my divorce or most subjects at all. I haven't had any dating disasters . . . yet.

INGRID: I have some doozies. It has made for some good stories.

ME: Oh, by the way, I lied about my age, height, and body type.

INGRID: How old are you REALLY?

ME: 45, and I've lost A LOT of hair since those photos. No longer a horse's mane.

INGRID: I actually have slightly darker hair now (really). Hope that's not a deal breaker.

ME: Ugh, really?

INGRID: Yes, really, you jerk!

ME: I was teasing.

INGRID: I know.

ME: Your day is over?

INGRID: I'm still working and then I'm meeting a friend for a drink in Williamsburg (ugh) at 7:30. So now I have to kill time. What are you up to tonight?

ME: I'm not sure. Maybe staying in. I have a packed day tomorrow. Brunch with a friend, then a reading that seems like it may go on forever, and then a going-away party.

INGRID: Brunch! Where?

ME: I'm not sure. I'm tagging along with a friend to be a buffer for another friend.

INGRID: Ah. Well, brunch is my favorite thing pretty much ever.

ME: Why exactly?

INGRID: I can't believe you're asking that. But, obviously:

1. Bacon
2. Sweet and savory combinations
3. WAFFLES
4. Maple syrup and butter

5. Many drinks (coffee AND juice!? crazy!)
6. It's relaxing
7. Often outdoors

ME: But that can be breakfast as well.

INGRID: True. What do you have against brunch? This is very upsetting.

ME: So much.

1. The neologism
2. Deciding between lunch and breakfast
3. Crowds
4. The national deficit

How many did you have? I don't have seven in me. The coffee isn't working anymore.

INGRID: This is quite the revelation. What if I took you somewhere that wasn't crowded and we went early enough that it could be considered breakfast? And it was TASTY?

ME: You are some kind of magical problem-solver.

INGRID: I just can't live in a world where people don't love brunch. It's too sad.

ME: No, I love brunch. How long have you worked at the museum?

INGRID: A little over six months, so not long.

ME: And you like it?

INGRID: I love it! It's such a fun place to work. Everyone's lovely, it's great to be working for an institution I believe in and care about, blah blah.

ME: Did you go to school for art?

INGRID: No, no, no. I majored in journalism and dramatic literature.

ME: Dramatic literature as in studying texts, or acting out the texts?

INGRID: Studying. Not acting. God, no. That would be my worst nightmare.

ME: I was hoping that was the answer.

INGRID: Don't worry, I'm not some kind of theater nut.

ME: You so are. We should go see *Hairspray*. Or have you already, like, five times?

INGRID: No, no, I have not.

ME: It is okay if that is where you're salary goes too.

INGRID: Oh, brother.

ME: Is that because of my typo?

INGRID: Ha! No, I was feigning annoyance at you giving me grief.

ME: I know. I was being sassy.

INGRID: Sass doesn't always come across well on chat when you haven't yet met the person.

ME: I know sass doesn't, but what is weird is that I like that it doesn't come across.

INGRID: Why's that?

ME: I'm not sure. I think it is the confusion of language and tone, and that it highlights or provides proof that it is difficult to communicate. Like, here I am trying to be myself and it fails, and that feels like a big DUH to me. And it is reassuring.

INGRID: I'm totally picking up on your sass, I'm just giving you a hard time (sassing back).

ME: I just got played. Is that what you are saying?

INGRID: Yes. Well, you didn't get played, but YOU weren't picking up on MY sass. You can pretty much always assume I'm sassing.

ME: Wait, could you point to the sass in the above text?

INGRID: I don't know, I guess I wasn't sassing that much.

ME: You have an awesome name btw.

INGRID: Oh, thank you! You have a lovely name yourself (<-- not sass).

ME: Thanks. Fletcher is my mother's last name. That is why I use it.

INGRID: The three-name thing is hard to pull off, but you do it with aplomb.

ME: I made a choice to use it a while ago. What is your middle name?

INGRID: Holly (meh).

ME: Holly Scott works nice though.

INGRID: Yeah, but Ingrid > Holly. I'm much more of an Ingrid. You haven't met me yet, you'll see.

ME: Ok, am I going to meet you? I forget.

INGRID: No, actually, I'd prefer to just have a relationship over chat, if that's okay.

ME: Deal. I think that might work better for me too.

INGRID: So what time is good for you on Sunday?

ME: Whenever. I have nothing planned.

INGRID: I'm just going to say this once, because I don't want you to get on a high horse, but you are quite a dish.

ME: Aw, I just blushed.

INGRID: Ha!

ME: I blush easy though. Skin tone and all.

INGRID: Oh god, I'm half girl, half-beet. So pale, the slightest blush is noticeable.

ME: I'm a ghost.

INGRID: Oh my god, what if you were ACTUALLY a ghost? If only.

My first post-marriage kiss was initiated over instant message—I'd been on four dates with Bella and there had been brief hand holding. Knees touched once while we sat on a bench by the Hudson River as the sun set or we sat waiting for the sun to set, and there were four long goodbye hugs—my face turned from hers, eyes wide, my heart beating in proportion to my perspiration. I'm an adult. I was thinking too much. It had been months since I'd kissed someone, and then years before I kissed someone different, kissed differently. A peck on the check. Mouth slightly ajar. Bottom lip in my mouth. Dry. Wet. Bad breath. It is a moment invested with superstition and drama, and almost utterly inconsequential—we learn to kiss our partners over time, in one long night. The first kiss is only to say, "Yes," "I want to kiss you," "I just kissed you," "What's next?"

It was middle school all over again. Beth Warner standing against the brick wall, yellow buses around the corner—it was awkward, pressured. We'd been dating since Christmas, maybe I bought her a charm bracelet from Woolworth's—I couldn't afford Macy's. It was quick. It was over. Her braces had been removed three days before and I watched her swipe her new teeth with her tongue. She didn't tell me it was good. Didn't congratulate me with a gold star or ever kiss me again. I was an adult now. I understood the basic mechanics.

Nina had first kissed me in the stairwell to my apartment, without warning. She was in the process of breaking up with someone and though we flirted via email throughout the workday the thought of anything happening hadn't entered my mind as a real possibility since the barrier of a relationship hadn't yet been removed, even if I knew its disintegration was imminent. Of course, I was quick with critical words towards her current boyfriend, providing a near constant litany of ways in which he was unappreciative, downright rude, and bordering on complete assholeness, whenever the opportunity seemed to naturally present itself. He wouldn't let her spend the night and called a cab at three in the morning. "Really, what kind of person would do that?" She told me both his parents were deaf and he'd never learned sign language. "Really, what kind of person wouldn't want to be able to communicate with their parents?" I was a passive-aggressive advocate for a more understanding partner—I was the new boy sending emails signed "xoxo."

I typed the following eloquent sentence into the IM box, because as with most things, it was easier than talking about it face to face.

ME: Hey, so is it weird we haven't, you know, like done anything yet?

BELLA: What are you talking about?

ME: I mean if you just think of me as a friend that is completely cool, and no pressure or anything.

BELLA: Oh, you mean, like made-out yet?

When she arrived at my apartment that night to watch *Deadwood*, I paused in the lobby and kissed her. Her lips didn't quite part, and my mouth was too eager. It never went further than that.

By the time I met Ingrid, I had recently shared nine first kisses (receptionist at a hair salon, two elementary school teachers, an architecture student, a bartender, a nanny, two librarians, an assistant at a PR firm), and the hurdle of crippling self-doubt about when and how and is this person actually attracted to me had become such a normal question as to be a question I allowed myself to ignore. On our first date, after three hours at the café on the walk back to my apartment, I leaned over and kissed Ingrid as we waited for the crosswalk light to change. The idea was to appear natural.

Dear Mom,

With these letters, what I find myself asking for or, rather, requiring, in order to even have a semblance of a relationship with you—more meaningful than opening your cards and jotting a thank you note, or phone calls every month and a half with a report on who is doing what and with who and where—is an apology. By an apology I do not mean a defense, an excuse, a life history of events crafting a psychological profile, but an acknowledgement of wrongdoing regardless of intent. "A fearless, moral inventory of wrongs, and a willingness to make amends."

I find this necessary to dwell on because we never have. I am not responsible. I won't be. I tell myself: *You cannot parent the parent.* I am responsible for myself. I've been sober thirteen years. As the estranged son, left with information passed from one brother to another like a game of whisper-down-the-lane, I hear information revised as each imagination interprets the events for the other. I mishear their reports as: "She must live with herself." I tell my brothers: "I never asked for much." They tell me: "Ask for less." You're unable to reach out to me. I should be bigger. "If she were sick with cancer you wouldn't turn your back."

I've never made it easy for you. I was distant, and on the phone I was short. I never asked: "How are Mittens and Professor Booty?" We could have at least talked about our pets. I never told you how I calculated the time it takes for my cats to follow me into bed. (On average, thirty seconds to a minute.) At any hour of day, they jump from the top of the bookcase or refrigerator, or drift from inside the closet to come lay beside me. I can't help thinking there is something pathetic in these calculations. I don't want to feel dependent and yet I am. On unlocking the door and walking up the stairs I anticipate their meowing behind the door. It provides comfort. On the phone you would ask: How are things? "Fine." Enter silence.

If, on the contrary, I had demonstrated any sign of openness, you might have made the first gesture. And now, I've moved forward in life without this relationship, and it's a defining element for how I've come to view myself in the world. The glass half-full and emptying, the disappointment around the corner. To that end, what would reconciliation entail? What if we sat down, face to face, and talked? Who would I be then?

Noah says your gestures of reconciling are like a meteor traveling through the atmosphere burning away its mass until it lands to earth as a pebble in a field unnoticed as part of the natural landscape. Simon tells me you asked: "Is he just not talking to the family?" I tell them: "Tell her I will not speak with her until she apologizes." They tell me, "Tell her yourself."

Love,
Brett

I don't know what I was looking for searching Nina's name online—an inevitable wedding announcement, a wedding registry? Each time I searched, I prepared myself, took the prerequisite deep breath for what I might uncover, for the moment of shock, my stomach finding new and unbearable ways to contort. I asked myself if it would be better or worse to discover that Nina ended up marrying Richard, by which I mean better or worse as to how I would interpret the event, the version of the narrative I would create and live with. I knew a marriage would serve to legitimatize her actions—that the pain and suffering she caused me and Richard's wife would now in some regards become justified: star-crossed lovers, soulmates who were meant for each other and found themselves in complicated situations but prevailed over their circumstances in order to experience true love. I wondered how they would tell any future children they might have or for that matter anyone, how they met. "We met at work." Would their children and colleagues know they were married before? Would their children care? And why did I care about their future offspring or cocktail party friends? I thought about the moments in which they might feel compelled to disclose their actions and how they had contextualized it to their loved ones, and hoped those moments were awkward for everyone.

If they were to get married, would it be a small wedding on a beach or at the courthouse? I wondered if my friends would tell me, if they would know, if they were still in touch with her. Maybe I was ahead of myself, I didn't even know if they were living with each other, if they had already combined their two homes with all the appliances and gadgets after our divorce. I went to the Macy's website and searched their names in the wedding registry—they would certainly need to replace some things, items get worn down, two-households-to-one or not. New sheets, for instance. Even if they weren't the jealous types and nothing lingered in the other's mind when one of them stayed at work late, it might just be common courtesy not to fuck on the sheets you fucked your previous husband or wife on.

I wondered if Nina would purchase items I hadn't been interested in. She had wanted Fiestaware dishes the first time we walked through Macy's with a price gun, giddy and scanning items to a virtual wish list. I wasn't a fan. The colors seemed particular to a California upbringing, and I wanted to resist this. I knew we were moving to California in a few months and thought I had conceded too much already and resisted embracing too fully the domestic landscape of a California kitchen, which the pottery came to represent. I'm sure Richard was a better man, or maybe they shared the same taste, or he didn't have a strong aesthetic vision for his life. Maybe he hated Fiestaware but would compromise: "You can have the canisters, but not the dish set." Maybe such compromise hinted at a long and healthy marriage.

When I moved into my apartment, I didn't think of it as a bachelor pad per se, but I did think there was the prospect, however far off, that someone else might stay the night there with me. I wanted the best of everything. I told myself I deserved it—that, having left almost everything in California, sleeping on cheap thin sheets would only add to my depression. I wanted small details of my apartment to combine with other small details towards a collective home. I wanted to feel like I wasn't a sad divorcé with mismatched items. I went to Home Depot to replace the plastic light switchplates and electrical sockets with a brushed metal variety. I bought a ceramic dish for the kitchen sponge, a device that stored all my grocery bags and attached to the door below the sink, and lavender-scented hand soap. More importantly, it was about feeling at home, creating a place with purpose rather than a place of necessity—i.e. a room I needed to rent because my wife no longer wanted me. These were items that displayed care, thoughtfulness. And in the end, I knew this wasn't for me. It was anticipating that someone would one day walk up the stairs and into the hallway, and see my apartment, superficially or not, as a reflection of who I was.

I told myself if I found a registry for Nina and Richard, I would purchase the most expensive item on it for them as a gift. I would start a Kickstarter campaign asking friends and strangers for donations in order to purchase a set of twelve crystal goblets, a Dyson vacuum. I wasn't sure it was worth the joke, but it might be how we should utilize the Internet: small donations and micro-loans for jokes. It is possible I only contemplated this not from real vengeance, but in order to have the story to retell later.

Ingrid had the best laugh, loud and long, pure and goofy. She was filled with a joy that was infectious—it was found in a cat in a brownstone window, paintings, old soul records, puns, lord did she love puns. All of this without being a Pollyanna—she had an edge and bitterness, but wasn't world-weary. She was the first person I dated whom I introduced to friends, who came to a work event. Why in the world did she allow me to ironically wear a pink trucker hat the first time I met her friends? Or ever? What was I thinking? What were they thinking? There are no excuses, and yet maybe she was too shy or possessed a certain sense of decorum that prohibited her mocking my fashion choices, or maybe it was some ridiculous quirk she found charming.

My friends began adding her to email chains almost immediately—I'm not sure they even asked me—inviting her to poetry readings, to kids' birthday parties, where incidentally all the children swarmed her, pulling her arms to show her a new doll, to create a new imaginary world. Even my neighborhood welcomed her. The men who were forever outside my door on a upside-down milk crate reading the paper, scratching a lotto ticket, observing our coming and goings, the neighbors who had renamed me "David Spade," now just pointed and said "Here come the movie stars." It was a welcome change for me; we laughed, and I gave a cigarette to anyone who asked to bum one.

One day when I entered the laundromat where I deposited my thirty-pound bag of clothes to be washed each week, the women working there became excited. They began laughing, talking to each other, and pointing towards me and then to the bag I'd come to pick up. Tied to the outside of bag, where once they had tied a key I had left in a pocket of a pair of jeans, were a few of Ingrid's intimate items, carefully folded. She had left them at my apartment. The women knew they weren't mine. They'd not only become familiar with me, but with my belongings. And now here we all stood, not sharing a common language, attempting to get to the bottom of this mystery. They were unclear if they had suddenly uncovered a secret habit or, as happens occasionally, an errant item left over in the dryer from the previous customer's load had mistakenly wound up with my items. I blushed; it is something with my pale skin that I excel at, blushing. I stammered "Oh! Oh, no. No," trying to string together an explanation. I stepped outside where Ingrid was waiting; I pulled her toward the open doorway and pointed at her. Ingrid raised her hand, an accounting for, a wave. The women immediately understood.

It was easy and it was natural with Ingrid. I don't mean "easy" in the sense that we both liked chicken pot pie and so unwrapped the frozen pot pie cellophane together and placed them in the microwave and settled down on the couch just in time to watch our stories, forevermore. And I don't mean "natural" to hint at the notion of soulmates locating each other in a world filled with unlimited choices and false turns. What I mean is that I felt like myself, that though maybe there is excitement and drama in playing roles, ultimately a life of such constant performance isn't sustainable. And the excitement she felt for the world didn't necessarily open my eyes, but it allowed me to remember those aspects of myself.

The first period of estrangement from my mother when I was a teenager concluded in classic subterfuge, with Noah employing the oldest trick in the book. It is a trick, I understand, only successful when both parties willingly, perhaps even subconsciously, allow themselves to be misled, from hubris and a stubborn unwillingness to admit their errors, and ultimately with the desire to be reconciled. "He would like to see you." "She would like to see you." He told me she had stopped drinking. Five years of relative silence ended based on misinformation. I walked down a corridor to a person standing in the doorway, as if nothing had transpired. We hugged. She said: "I'm glad you came."

I felt alienated from my brothers then, and that feeling seems even more pronounced for this latest go-round of refusing to speak to my mother. I imagine that they think I'm unwilling to accept or respect an opinion different than my own. I was the last to be born; a decade separates me from my oldest brother. It is the curse that the role of the youngest child is to be forever the youngest, and thus what's seen as being principled is interpreted as disdainful righteousness—the preserving and naive ideals of a teenager who believes he understands perfectly the complexities of the adult world. I was twelve when my parents' divorce was finalized and Simon was six hours away at college. We set patterns to be meticulously adhered to and here I am, like a teenager again, the only son not speaking to his mother.

It is possible—it is quite likely—that my brothers' memories are different than mine. It should go without saying. I asked Simon what his earliest memory of the family was. It was early in the morning. I told him I wanted to interview him. We were drinking coffee. He was doing *The Philadelphia Inquirer's* Sunday crossword puzzle. I placed the recorder I purchased the night before between us. I started the recorder. "Philadelphia, December 15, 2007. What is your first memory?" He looked up. "Mom was crowning me." He turned off the recorder. He told me a different story about when I was born and he walked into my room, stood over the crib, and vowed to always take care of me. These days, I speak infrequently with any of my brothers. "Have you spoken to Dad? Have you spoken to Mom?" "I got nothing." "Yeah, me either." "Talk to you soon."

May 22, 2008
2:22 PM

ME: I saw you online on Nerve today. How is that working out for you?

INGRID: Ha!! Well, you were online too, then, weren't you?

ME: Yeah, I was. I went to check to see if you were. Right?

INGRID: Yeah right. I got an email that someone had messaged me.

ME: Was she cute?

INGRID: Ha! I felt bad, because it was someone I'd been writing before I met you, and he sent me a very sad "Why haven't you written me back?" email.

ME: Oh, those suck!

INGRID: Yeah. I feel terrible. I don't want to lead him on.

ME: How many emails back and forth did you have?

INGRID: Two each I guess?

ME: How many does it take to get you on a date?

INGRID: Depends. If I'm really interested I'll just go ahead and ask right away, but it depends on how the conversation is progressing. Like if the first email is one sentence, that doesn't really count for much. Do you remember how quickly I replied? I was all over that.

ME: I guess I do! So are you coming over tonight?

Dear Mom,

I will be turning thirty soon and next month would have been my third wedding anniversary. I should be shopping for the perfect gift made of leather. A journal bound in Italian leather, or luggage. A modern gift would be crystal or glass. A paperweight with a decoupage image of a French playing card, the ace of hearts frozen inside.

I won't attempt to draft an incomplete list of my likes and dislikes in an effort to get to know each other better. I'm unable to visualize the benefits; would we know what to cook if the other was coming for dinner? Too many days have come and gone, each one the same, each one slightly different, the weather on a yearly loop. It has rained for three straight weeks. It's strange the things I don't know about you. How many siblings did your mother have? I always forget. I know it approaches the double digits, maybe there were twins. Or what did you do the summer you lived in New York? Did you really work in a department store or have I invented that fact? I don't know when or how you met my father. I was never told. How many times can a history be repeated? I never asked. I was the fourth son, clearly the last hope for a daughter. By the time little league or piano lessons came around, both you and my father were exhausted with almost a decade of child-rearing. I would not be forced to play. I don't blame you. There is only so much stamina exerted before one gives in. It's these types of details I want, details that transform a character from a novel into someone almost real.

From my journal, October 1988: "Life at my house is painful. My brother Paul always picks on me because I am smaller. My brother Simon is my favorite brother, but he is away at college. My only brother left is Noah and he is never home or he is asleep. It's also hard because I hardly see my mom, but I sleep over at her house just about every weekend. But when I get home the only one I can do something with is my Dad but he is usually at a meeting or tutoring, but he is always there when I need him."

We can return to the beginning, to follow how things progressed. I recently found this form from preschool filled out by you or my father. I can't distinguish the handwriting. I look at the cards you sent me over the years, filled with celebratory slogans: "Happy Birthday" and "Merry Christmas." There isn't enough handwriting to create a sample size to compare adequately. I tell myself though, that the handwriting on the form is yours—that we're sitting at the kitchen table, where my homework was done, where my school projects were glued together and sprinkled with glitter, where we lived together, an unhappy family similar to all unhappy families, hoping things could change, and waiting as they didn't. There shouldn't be anything special about it.

Dear Parents,

We are eager to get to know your child and have him feel important and happy coming to school. To foster this we would like you to discuss with your child these things of interest about himself/herself. Please write the response on this sheet. Do not feel pressured to fill in every blank. Do feel free to add any comments of your own or your child's.

Please bring this autobiography with you to the interview.

My name is Brett. I am 5 years old. My favorite toy is my boat. I like to eat cake and chicken. The other people who live at our house are: Dad, Mom, Noah 11, Simon 13, Paul 8, Logan (dog), fish, and the hamster.

Something else I want you to know about me is: I don't care.

At William Penn Center I hope I will be able to: Learn to read.

General Health: Brett is in excellent health, although slightly small for his age. He had a milk allergy as a baby and consequently will not drink milk. He does however eat milk products, i.e. cheese, ice cream.

General Knowledge: Brett has learned much from his brothers. He likes to look at books and magazines and can usually find someone to answer his questions. He also formulates his own theories.

Interest and Behavior: Brett seems to deal well with both peers and adults. He has begun to take the lead in playing with his friends. He likes to dig holes, build forts, set up army men and play super heroes.

Goals for This School Year: We'd like to have Brett make continued progress—learn his abc's and maintain his positive attitude toward school.

I can best describe my child by saying: He's a pretty good all around kid.

Comments: His older brothers are concerned about possible WWIII, talk army etc. a lot. Brett picks up their lead.

Can define:

    Ball: A circle.

    Lake: I don't know.

    House: Has a Roof.

    Ceiling: Where light is.

    Jumps from bottom step: Yes.

    Hops 2 times on 1 foot: Needs support.

    Balances on one foot for 5 seconds: Needs support.

Brett enjoys being independent. He has fit into our routine very well. He prefers speaking to grown-ups. He has a quiet voice and is difficult to understand at times. He is also reluctant to speak in group situations. He dresses for outdoor activities but needs help with buttons. He accepts responsibility, but cries easily. He needs improvement showing concern and sympathy. He has difficulty holding a pencil.

Love,
Brett

The summer my mother kicked us all out of the house, Noah was the first to make amends, to return to her a day or two later. It was the end of summer, he was returning to college in Washington, DC. He needed a ride, or my mother had previously promised him a coffee table or a dresser for his new apartment. Or he had other emotional reasons. And then at my wedding, Noah was the first to comfort her, to follow her to the gravel parking lot, to stop an immediate and stormy exit. She stayed through the first toast, in which Simon read a childhood poem of mine.

After my wedding, Simon didn't speak with my mother for a month, not an abnormal amount of time to pass in our family. I can't be sure if his distance was meant to pass judgment on her behavior or not. As a teenager, Simon had been my silent partner when she had kicked us out of the house. He went three years without communicating with her, and then one day he slipped a note under my bedroom door.

Dear Brett,

I'm sorry that you are so mad at me. I know you don't like what I'm doing and I understand your point of view and how you feel. I never meant to let you down or make you feel alone. It doesn't really matter if I talk to Mom now or five years from now. It's something I have to do. I know that may sound selfish to you. In the end, everyone must find their own happiness and do what they think is right—be an individual. One of the greatest things about you is that you are an individual and try to live by what you know is right in your heart. I totally respect that about you. But in my heart I know that I must at least talk to Mom again one day in my life. I know you don't understand me but that is honestly how I feel. Nobody is perfect. We all make mistakes, including mom and myself. No matter how hard we try, it is nearly impossible to make ourselves or anyone else perfect. Don't put so much pressure on yourself to be absolutely perfect. You have friends that care about you and a family that loves you, including your brother and Dad. I care about you so much and hate to see you so mad and upset. You are a great person. I know you try very hard to please everybody and to do the right thing. I am very proud of you and I love you very much. We will always be brothers (even if you wish we weren't). We may not always agree or have the same views, but as long as I'm around you will never be alone. I'll always be there for you and you can always trust me and count on me to take care of you. You are my kid brother and one of my favorite people in the world. I love you very much. Hang in there "little man."

Simon

Dear Mom,

It causes me great pain to confront you with this letter. None of this has been addressed since I was twelve and now I am thirty. I will feel guilt when you die, that you will die without your youngest son. But that guilt seems a selfish reason to speak with you.

I didn't want to accept your letters or your holiday checks. It was a weakness. I wanted to demonstrate an understanding of right and wrong, both to myself, and to you. Gestures are noticed in the world. Your monthly bank statement noted the check was cashed. By cashing them, I continued to have contact with a person I refused to have contact with.

I knew when I was twelve and I know it now, that it was unprincipled to allow you to reach me. I don't want to be found, located, and understood. I have given up trying to forgive you. Maybe I'm supposed to rise to the occasion. As a child, my observational skills were not yet enriched with the knowledge of the particulars of the disease and I was lucky that my own addiction ended without any serious or irreparable damage to myself or others. But now I should know better, should have the empathetic understanding that the rooms of addiction and recovery should have instilled.

Instead I will address this letter, seal it, and place it in the box beneath my bed.

I hear a pigeon cooing on the fire escape. If it is white, my luck will change. I will forget this all tomorrow or attempt to memorialize it.

Dear Mom, I got nothing. Talk to you soon?

Love,
Brett

June 3, 2008
10:35 AM

INGRID: I feel terrible about our conversation last night. You've been so lovely, and I'm totally happy with things as they are.

ME: You don't have to feel terrible about anything.

INGRID: I was just in a little bit of a mood yesterday and I'm sorry if I said anything hurtful or annoying.

ME: Nah, hold on.

INGRID: Ok, I'm going to keep typing anyway—I just feel dumb for being such a girl. You're not really being distant at all. I'm just feeling vulnerable because I like you, so I'm anxious for any kind of reciprocal "I like you, too" gesture. I just need to chill and I can. Ok. That's what I wanted to say.

ME: Well, a) I don't want you selling yourself short about what you want and expect because you are easy-going, passive, or "selfless" b) You shouldn't feel that you have to back-step after expressing yourself, I'm a big dude, a huge dude, and can deal with it.

INGRID: Meh, I was just thinking it over on my own. Plus, as I'm sure you noticed, I was so sleepy when we were having that conversation. I wasn't in the best state of mind.

ME: I actually think your points were valid.

INGRID: Well, what do you think about all this now? In the light of day.

ME: I am VERY angry.

INGRID: What? Really? At me?

ME: Oh come on!

INGRID: Well, I don't know. You said you didn't feel good about the conversation, that could mean anything.

ME: I'm concerned about certain things.

INGRID: Ok, what specifically?

ME: Your generation wants to deal with everything on chat . . . just kidding.

INGRID: We can wait and talk in person.

ME: My understanding is this: You want to feel secure with me, and I am a little distant, I will admit that, it is a way to protect myself from being vulnerable, yet in order for you to feel secure I will need to be vulnerable, and for me to be able to see and get to know the whole Ingrid package, I will need to be vulnerable so you feel secure expressing yourself.

INGRID: I'd say that's spot-on. So now what do we do? What do you want at this point? I don't want to feel like I'm forcing you to do something that makes you uncomfortable.

ME: I do have a question though.

INGRID: Yes?

ME: I'm looking for a working definition or clarification of how all these terms work. Would you say you are dating me? Seeing me? If you said it is "casual" what does that mean, if each person isn't seeing anyone else? And if each person isn't seeing anyone else, what is that?

INGRID: Oh. Yeah, I don't know, those terms are all so vague.

ME: Well, how do you use them?

INGRID: I think everyone has different definitions. I guess I would say I was either dating you or seeing you. I think of those as being basically the same thing. Meaning, we're not officially bf/gf.

ME: Now again, what does that "not officially" mean?

INGRID: Official = had a discussion about it, acknowledging that it's serious, not dating anyone else, etc. I think that's pretty standard. I think it just depends on what the two people agree on, it's always a gray area. I'd say not official means not fully committed or exclusive, like, right now, for instance, you could be dating other people, and that would be okay, because you'd be totally within your rights. That doesn't mean I'd be thrilled about it but it would be fine, morally. I'm sure other people feel differently about it.

ME: Gotcha. But shouldn't the fact that it would make you unhappy affect what you would want or ask for?

INGRID: Right, but at this point, having agreed to not be exclusive; I wouldn't really have any right to be upset. Of course I'm entitled to feel whatever I feel.

ME: Ok. Any questions for me?

INGRID: I guess I'm just wondering how you're feeling about all this in general? Are you freaking out? I don't want you to feel uncomfortable or like I'm putting any pressure on you.

ME: First, I don't think you are putting any pressure on me. I can handle that.

INGRID: Okay.

ME: But what are you asking me? How I feel about you? How I feel about dating?

INGRID: I meant the first one, but both I guess.

ME: I like hanging out with you. You make me feel good and comfortable and sexy. I want to spend time with you and get to know you better, and look forward to seeing you, and all those things seem like good signs. Is that bad?

INGRID: No! It's great.

ME: Is there something else you wanted me to be thinking?

INGRID: No! Not at all I just wanted to make sure I was interpreting things right. I feel the same way.

ME: So you know, I'm not seeing anyone else, and if you are that is completely fine.

INGRID: I'm not. Would you really be fine with that? I don't want to, I'm just curious.

ME: I'm not saying it would make me feel amazing, but since I have obvious commitment issues, I just expect that it is a very real understandable possibility that someone wouldn't want to stake that much interest in that arrangement.

INGRID: Well, I have no qualms about being serious and no qualms about not being serious.

We were in bed, looking at my high school yearbook. I was bragging. Ingrid hadn't believed I was voted "Best Dressed." We made a handshake bet. I forget what for. A fancy chocolate bar, or the loser would have to go downstairs to pay the delivery man when he arrived with our food. A car, even though I can't drive. I hadn't mentioned that the subtitle to the award was actually "Most Likely to Be Seen on a Paris Runway." That sounded better, obviously, but it also offered an explanation at how the student body had arrived on my name through the popularity contest that is any high school voting. The specifics of a "Paris Runway" twisted their arms into selecting a slight weirdo in a disco-era butterfly collar and bell-bottoms rather than the boy in a polo shirt and khakis with perfectly parted hair.

Ingrid asked if we had met in high school whether we would have been friends. She wished she had known High School Brett. She joked that she was going to write and post a Missed Connection for my teenage self. She thought I should keep writing them, and should start a website cataloging the fake Missed Connections I'd been writing. I told her how tired I was of writing them.

She told me about "Take Care of Yourself," a recent work by the French artist Sophie Calle that was based on a break-up email the artist received and named after the last words in the correspondence. For the work, Calle had gathered responses to the offending email by 107 females who were experts in their field—a copyeditor proofed the letter, a cruciverbalist created a crossword puzzle of the words, a scientist and Talmudic scholar offered analysis. We began to brainstorm together, and settled on the idea that we should ask others to write the Missed Connections. We knew artists, musicians, and writers who would be willing to join the experiment. My boredom wasn't necessarily with the idea, but with the private obsessiveness, the tunnel vision of my particular experience, which was exhausting and exhausted. But, as with Calle's work, what can be interesting is another's particular version of loneliness, or how they imagine loneliness is articulated. As with a theatrical production, each actor invents his or her own backstory and motivation for a new run of an old play.

I showed Ingrid more photos, showed her Beth Warner, who was my first kiss, the girls I had wanted to date, and the boys who at various moments wanted to beat the shit out of me. I showed her a page of thirty portraits, all in the identical formal garb of black dress or tux, and asked her to identify who she imagined was the most popular person based on their photograph. And confirming some deep truth about high school, she was never correct.

I am of the belief that most terrible news arrives with a phone call. I don't expect the alert of the death of a loved one to arrive via a text message, and yet I never answer my phone, since the entities that call these days are robot debt collectors, Sallie Mae, and the junior high school that erroneously believes I am the guardian of a boy named Alberto, and is concerned I didn't return their call about parent–teacher conferences. When my phone vibrates with an unknown number, I don't pick up, I google that number.

I was visiting my brother Noah in Oregon. Ingrid and I had been dating for a few months, and she was staying at my apartment cat-sitting. This time, when her name appeared on my caller ID, I did answer. I had been away for a few days and hadn't heard her voice. But the voice on the other end wasn't hers. It was a man. He told me he had dialed the most recently called number in the phone and that "Whoever's phone this is just had a seizure and the ambulance took her to the hospital." He worked at a grocery store in Park Slope and informed me which hospital the ambulance had taken her to.

There wasn't much I could do from across the country. I couldn't be there to comfort her, couldn't ask the doctors questions about whether she fainted or had a seizure, and what could have caused it. It had been 90 degrees in Brooklyn. Maybe she was dehydrated, had low blood sugar. I went online and messaged Ingrid's roommate. I called my friend Charlie so he could get on the train and head to the hospital. Ingrid hadn't mentioned having an illness or condition. My only information was secondhand from a grocery clerk and what I read on the WebMD entry on seizures and how long they lasted, what happened to the body, what were the causes. There was no real way of knowing what had happened. I sat anxiously on a couch states away.

A few hours passed before her roommate called me. He handed the phone over to Ingrid, who was resting in the hospital with a bandage on her head, stuck with an IV injecting salt- and sugar-rich fluid, and in my memory, this is the first time she told me she loved me. Her roommate quickly took the phone from her—knowing it was still early in the relationship and protecting her from woozy talk. I said it back. It was the first time I had said it in a long time.

And I hate to tell this story this way, fearing it sounds like a relationship created from the bond of crisis or trauma. I imagine two people who meet in shared grief at a funeral, or over an existential crisis about humanity, like the thousands who must have been brought together after September 11 all over the city, the two old lovers who called each other to check in, to say "I was a fool, I'm standing outside your apartment door right now. Please let me in."

This was different. Instead of calling into question my own fragility, my own grief at an unknown future alone, it cut the emotional distance I was maintaining. This wasn't about my own selfish concerns or existential dread. It sounds so simple, so obvious; it was about experiencing the care and love I felt for another in my life. After the end of my marriage, this was something I had been unable to allow myself—up until this moment.

A greeting card arrived from my mother with a remorseful cartoon bear wearing a blue shirt and red slacks and a maze between
him and another bear.

"Here I am, there you are."

Dear Mom,

I don't know what to do. I'm not sure how to reach you. I searched last night and couldn't find your phone number. Is it possible I no longer have your number? I wonder if it is listed. We can go on like this forever, each searching for the other somewhere. Each asking Simon, Noah, Paul for information, facts, gauging the temperature of the other. And it is possible we might. I'm not sure what it means to have a mother, and by the same token, not to have one. You were always there, a phantom possibility things could be different. This is what absence taught me, that there is no absence. It will never be the same; it will happen all over again. Nothing grows fonder. It rots, it decays, is rebuilt over a burial ground. Now, as has always been the case, each morning begins where the night trailed off. There is no end. There is no beginning. The sun goes down and rises on the same set of grievances we invent and if nothing changes then nothing changes.

At a certain point I found myself standing in the line at Baskin-Robbins, wondering if the ice cream cake would fit the message I wanted to place on it. I brought it home to surprise Ingrid. Everyone loves cake. Everyone loves ice cream. I asked the person at the counter to write on the cake: "Will you be my girlfriend?" She looked at me and said: "Yes, if you brought me home this cake." And I brought home the cake, and that is how it started over. There has to be a moment—a grand or, in my case, a simple, ridiculous gesture, to say *Yes, I believe life with you will be better than life without you.*

And now, as I write this letter, Ingrid is asleep in the room to my left. She has read everything I have written so far in my memoir, copyedited, cut, insisted on changes and details, and it is better for it. I am better for the thinking she required of me. She knows everything now. One evening, as she slept, I saw a peaceful ghost-like figure hovering above her body as I sat here writing.

I've told myself it appeared again, after months, to investigate, to give the all-clear, to approve of my decisions. I haven't told her this yet. I've learned my lesson. Some things might be too early to reveal.

There is a black cat resting on her chest. It is my cat. The cat's name is Kiki. Ingrid takes more photographs of the cats than I do. She is allergic and at the beginning of each week she must wake early before work and take a train to the allergist to receive a shot that they hope will make her immune. She does this for me. She does this for the cats. I love that her emotions show on her face when she is unhappy. That she can express them. That she can challenge me when I'm wrong and I want to apologize. She has asthma, and I've had to stop smoking in the house. I would never want to hurt her. I must quit smoking soon. I love that on the street a dog, almost any dog, can bring her happiness, and that she knows the breeds of these dogs, the names of flowers, and every answer to the 90s edition of Trivial Pursuit. I love that she told me, after the fact, that when she entered my apartment for the first time that it was as if she decorated it herself. She only objects to a single band of color on the kitchen arch-way, painted in the ridiculous color Hot Lips. I love that she understands I couldn't not paint it Hot Lips. I love that she doesn't flinch when my step-mom accidently calls her Nina, that later that night when we whisper in the guest room, she doesn't launch into a list of complaints about the event, which she would be completely justified in doing, and I would understand, but that we can commiserate about it, turn it into something funny. And I love that she is excited to meet you, even or especially knowing that it might not be the easiest homecoming—we are still planning to visit over the Christmas break when Noah and Simon will be in town. I love that she has told me she's already reserved the email address ingridhollylauer@gmail.com and that she says "autumnal" as the season is changing.

Love always,
Brett

PERMISSIONS AND ACKNOWLEDGEMENTS

. . .

The instant message conversation with Bella reprints my side of the conversation, with Bella's words being recreated by Jennifer Kronovet without any knowledge or reference of Bella's original writing. Thanks to my father, Simon, Daphne, Charlie, Cassie, Jess, Mary, and Ingrid who all graciously granted permission to reprint their correspondences and writings. Some correspondence was combined and edited for grammar.

Sections of this book have appeared in *A Public Space*, *The Rumpus*, and on the Happy Ending Reading Series website. Thanks to Anthony Brosnan, Rob Casper, Timothy Donnelly, Monica Fambrough, Matthea Harvey, Stefania Heim, Rachelle Katz, Jenny Kronovet, Dan McGehean, Travis Nichols, Fred Nicolaus, Elsbeth Pancrazi, Peter Pihos, and of course my family. All my thanks in the world to Brigid Hughes, Lynn Melnick, and Gretchen Scott, who have read this book too many times and provided me with unlimited advice and wisdom. And thanks to Lindsay Edgecombe and Dan Smetanka.

Printed in the United States
by Baker & Taylor Publisher Services